Praise for

HEART
OF A L

D0835240

"This is a touching and uplifting true story about a boy named John Paul, who has half a heart but who lives with more heart and soul than just about any kid you will ever meet. John Paul rocks, and so does this book."

—**James Patterson,** *New York Times* best-selling author

"The story of John Paul George is absolutely amazing, just as his life has been. From before he was born to today, this young man has overcome all odds in the biggest game of all—the game of life. John Paul's is a great story of inspiration and perseverance and one I am sure you will want to read."

—**Jack Nicklaus,** golf legend

"John Paul's courageous story will instill hope and inspire you to believe that if your heart is open, you can prevail over insurmountable odds."

—**Jane Seymour,** actress

"John Paul is an awesome boy. His zest for life is contagious and his story an incredible read."

—**Ernie Els,** U.S. Open, British Open golf champion

"A devastating diagnosis inspires faith, hope, and fortitude as a family embarks on a journey to save their son. A heartwarming story which offers hope."

—**Chris Evert,** tennis legend

"John Paul's sparkling brown eyes and endearing smile radiate joy. This book radiates hope, love, and endurance."

—**Bill Parcells,** retired NFL head coach

"A story of a child who beat the odds. We hope to put a smile on your face. Go Big Blue."

—**The New York Giants**

"*Heart of a Lion* is a heartwarming and emotional true-life adventure involving a child's battle against formidable odds, his parents' unrelenting support, and help from higher sources."

—**Rob MacGregor,** author of
Indiana Jones and the Last Crusade

"An inspirational story of a family's relentless fight to save their son from a devastating diagnosis. Their journey inspires hope."

—**Alan Lavine** and **Gail Liberman,**
Dow Jones columnists and authors of
Quick Steps to Financial Stability

HEART
OF A LION

A Story of God's Grace and a Family's Hope

Derek and John Paul George

Liguori

Imprimi Potest:
Stephen Rehrauer, CSsR, Provincial
Denver Province, The Redemptorists

Published by Liguori Publications
Liguori, Missouri 63057

To order, call 800-325-9521 or visit Liguori.org.

Cataloging-in-Publication Data is on file with the Library of Congress

p ISBN: 978-0-7648-2545-3
e ISBN: 978-0-7648-6998-3

Except for the George family and public figures named herein, the names and places
of people and events have been changed.

Liguori Publications, a nonprofit corporation, is an apostolate of the Redemptorists.
To learn more about the Redemptorists, visit Redemptorists.com.

Printed in the United States of America
19 18 17 16 15 / 5 4 3 2 1
First Edition

To my wife, Annette, and our families,

I am thankful for the constant unending love and support.

Most of all, to John Paul, the love of my life;

you are my everything.

I thank God for blessing me with you.

About This Book

As a family, we do everything together, so it only seemed right that all three of us contribute to the new edition of this book. That's why you'll occasionally see sections that start with "from Annette" or "from John Paul," because I couldn't tell this story alone. John Paul will share what it's like being blessed with the miracle of life. Annette and I will share how God has gifted us with precious time with our son, time that wasn't supposed to be.

I remember a saying that Annette used to mimic from an old television series: *"Like sand through the hourglass, so are the days of our lives."*

The first time I heard Annette say that phrase, I asked exactly what that meant. She said it was the opening for a soap opera that had been on forever and explained the meaning from her point of view. She told me that we should take a minute and imagine the hourglass as our lives and each grain of sand as one day that we have to live. She continued to describe how quickly the sand falls through the hourglass and how within a blink of an eye the top part of the hourglass becomes empty. Before you know it, all the grains of sand are gone and so are our lives.

When you think about our time on earth from that perspective, it's an eye-opener. We are blessed each day to have our son with us.

***

"You can be born into a nightmare,
but God can usher you into a dream."

—Tyler Perry

Contents

Contents

Introduction

John Paul's story is one Annette and I have always wanted to share. By telling his story, our desire is to offer hope, faith, and comfort to others. The decision to write a book about John Paul goes back to the early months of his life. It was in the breezeway of the hospital where we waited that a vow was made. This was the one area of the hospital that wasn't cold or sustained by artificial lights and didn't feel like the walls were closing in on us. This breezeway offered an abundance of sunlight and views of the outside, so we gravitated to it. We sat on a cushion bench holding hands, silently praying, and hoping for positive news from the doctors about our son, John Paul.

Although waiting was something to which we had grown accustomed, it was still difficult to endure. Our conversation always revolved around John Paul. Annette and I talked about the many miracles God had bestowed on our son at this early stage of his life, but we were praying for one more. We thought of the many times we had been told there was no hope and the many times our hearts had been pierced by despair. We relied on our faith. What else were we going to do? We refused to give up, so we relied on our faith and prayed for miracles.

> *Merriam-Webster.com defines* **miracle** *as*
> *"an unusual or wonderful event that is believed*
> *to be caused by the power of God."*

John Paul's life is a miracle. There is no other way his life can be described. He isn't supposed to be here. He wasn't supposed to live beyond birth. There wasn't supposed to be hope. That was the unwavering consensus of doctors from prestigious medical institutions, whose assumptions were based on evidence. But they failed to consider one crucial factor: the power of God's divine intervention.

Sickness does not discriminate by age, race, or background, but neither do God's miracles. For those suffering, life can be a daily challenge and that suffering, although different in nature, filters through to all their family members.

Twenty years ago when John Paul was born, Annette and I were like deer caught in headlights. John Paul's condition was so rare that we often talked about how we wished there had been someone who could have given us insight into what to expect. Still, we quickly learned how to be advocates for our beliefs and for our son.

Some years ago, we took John Paul to a golf tournament. There was a family there whose young son had hypoplastic left heart syndrome, the same disease as John Paul. The parents had heard about John Paul and were excited to meet him. During the introductions, the mother of the young boy began to cry as she looked at John Paul smiling at her. She explained that her tears were tears of joy, because she now saw hope and a future for her son. For my family that's what it's all about, offering encouragement to parents and families with sick children or loved ones, or to those who are encountering obstacles of a different kind.

The journey has not been easy. Our lives have had many twists and turns. At certain times, the journey has mimicked a wild roller coaster ride, but the message we impart from that journey is positive and uplifting. Sometimes the deepest valley can lead us to a bountiful mountaintop.

One morning on my daily run, a lady stopped me and told me how she keeps John Paul's story on her nightstand. She explained that it remains there and has become her daily dose of inspiration. Isn't that what we all need? An evergreen story that continues to inspire no matter what your day holds?

God's encompassing love has given me my blessing, John Paul. He is our gift. We have learned not to take one day for granted. Each day is a blessing. People who come to visit our home are surprised when they walk in the door, because the first thing they spot is a Christmas tree. You may wonder why we display our Christmas tree year round. The answer comes easily. With John Paul in our lives, each and every day is like Christmas.

I vowed to share that gift and to share John Paul's miracles and God's grace; to proclaim our story of faith, hope, and encouragement to others; and, most importantly, to cherish the gift of life.

From John Paul

I am proud of my parents for sharing my story, but in order to help others, my voice should be heard too.

Through the story of my life, I hope others realize that no matter the obstacle God is always with us. In good times and bad, he remains our constant. Even when we are falling, God will help us up. We must not back down, we must not lose faith, and we must hold onto our cross and not let go.

We live in a society in which some feel the need to bully others because of the way they look, the way they live, or what they believe, among other things. I hope my story encourages those who bully to think twice before committing this awful act. To those who are suffering or who have suffered from the effects of bullying, my goal is to be an inspiration, so you can see that you are amazing just the way you are. We are all different and unique. God made us that way; that's what makes us special.

I am different because I live each day with a life-threatening disability. This is my cross, but I own it. I share my story so that others, no matter what they may be going through, can relate to certain feelings and catch that glimmer of hope. I have learned to deal with the struggle and fear of being different. I think many can identify with that. Living with half a heart is also not my only obstacle. I am very short for my age—most people think I'm eleven years old when in reality I am twenty. When I go into a restaurant, I'm still offered a kid's menu and crayons. These issues are difficult, but I own them and that's what makes me John Paul. I'm happy to be alive doing the will of God. I thank him for allowing me to be in the world and, hopefully, help others through the telling of my story.

I can't change who I am, but I can change the world as I am.

Prologue

I have lost count of the number of days that my wife Annette and I have stayed within the confines of this solemn environment. For us, time stands still. We are riding an emotional roller coaster, bouncing between hope and despair.

It is the end of June, but our daily routine hasn't changed since the birth of our son, John Paul, on June 4. Like most new parents, we remain vigilant at his bedside, but unlike most, we are praying, hoping, and waiting for any signs of improvement.

Our son's cardiologist, Dr. Renar, a woman in her late thirties, approaches us. "Go home," she says. "Get a good night's sleep so you'll be refreshed when John Paul wakes up."

These are the words of encouragement given to us by a doctor or nurse every day. The answer is always the same: "I can't leave because something might go wrong and I won't be around." But tonight, Dr. Renar is persistent. John Paul's condition is stable. I take her advice this time, still apprehensive about my son.

As I start to leave, I realize I'm not sure how to get out of the hospital. The building has become home. Annette and I have been maintaining a 24/7 vigil by our son. We walk hand in hand as we make our way to the bright-red exit sign, but the closer I get to the door the heavier my steps become. I feel guilty for leaving without my son in my arms.

Once home, the first thing that catches my attention is a car seat, the only baby purchase we made. Annette can't bear to look at the car seat. She avoids it and walks into the bedroom. I stand and stare. I envision buckling John Paul in for his first car ride.

We aren't able to sleep for long. Around midnight, the sound of a ringing phone pierces through the darkness. At the echo of the first ring, my stomach churns. The voice on the other end confirms my worst fear: John Paul has taken a turn for the worse. I don't remember getting dressed, but once behind the wheel of my car the adrenaline takes over. I whiz through every stop light and stop sign, flashing hazard lights. The car won't go fast enough.

We finally screech into a parking space and make a mad dash for the door. As soon as the florescent lights and hospital smells hit, the reality sets in. This may be the last time I see my son. We are in a race against time. Annette and I enter the pediatric intensive care unit (PICU). Doctors and nurses surround John Paul's tiny crib. Dr. Renar sees and approaches us; the look on her face says it all.

"John Paul's saturations are dropping fast. His brain and body are being starved for air. It is doubtful his heart will withstand the pressure." She states what no parent wants to hear, "John Paul only has a 1 percent chance of surviving."

Annette's body goes limp. I pull her toward me, trying to stay strong, but I feel I am at the end of my rope. *Why this innocent little boy? Why is he suffering like this? Is this how it's going to end? Is a parent's worst nightmare really happening to me?*

PART I

Come, Holy Spirit, fill the hearts of your faithful
and kindle in them the fire of your love.
Send forth your Spirit, and they shall be created.
And you shall renew the face of the earth.

Chapter 1

I was born in Benoni, South Africa, which is just twenty minutes outside of Johannesburg. The tropical climate is similar to south Florida, with the exception of it being a little cooler in the winter. The city has many tree-lined streets, parks, and numerous lakes, which is why it is called the City of Lakes. I grew up in a community known as Benoni Small Farms. Although the name implies I lived on a farm, I didn't. Actually, it was just a home in the country with acres of land but no livestock. There was plenty of room for my sister, brothers, and me to roam and have fun. When I was older, we moved to a quiet neighborhood in Benoni.

My parents have always been very devoted to their Catholic faith, which set a precedent for my brothers, my sister, and me. We all attended Mass regularly, and this foundation of my faith laid the groundwork for the things I stand for in my adult life: faith, family, respect, and determination. No matter the challenges, twists, or turns, I keep my focus on God and my faith, knowing that will lead me through.

One of my earliest memories as a child was of my brother Gary and his sickness. When Gary was born, he was very ill and spent a long time in the hospital. It was hard on my mom and dad trying to keep the household functioning while also tending to my sister and me. My mom and I traveled daily from Benoni to the hospital in Johannesburg. Children weren't allowed in the hospital, so I would have to stay in the car. There I waited patiently and always prayed for good news.

My brother did eventually get to come home, but he struggled for a big part of his childhood, especially during school. People would often pick on him. My parents taught me to watch out for my younger brother and to step in to avert the teasing, so that's exactly what I did. Gary made it through these obstacles too, and later in life even realized his calling to become a Catholic priest.

My calling was harder to distinguish. Tennis dominated my sports life and actually paved the way to my future. Before I could pursue those future plans, however, I had to serve two years in the South African Defense Force, which was mandatory after graduation from high school. In the army I became a physical training instructor, or PTI. As a PTI, I was in charge of the total fitness of the troops, which included mental, emotional, social, and physical elements. At the time, I regretted having to give away those two years of my life. It was only after the birth of my son that I realized how valuable the skills I learned as a PTI would be in helping John Paul overcome complications.

After completion of my mandatory service, I resumed tennis full-time and I was granted a full scholarship to Campbell University in North Carolina. That's where the interesting part of my future commenced.

It was summer when I met Annette in the school cafeteria. It was one of the first days of the semester. She was attending summer school to finish the one course she needed for graduation. I saw her eating supper with her friend, and my eyes remained fixed on her. She noticed my stare and sarcastically asked if I would like to take a picture, which would last longer, or come and have a seat. Not used to the American lingo of sarcasm, I truly thought she was inviting me over to talk with her. We often laugh about the entire scenario now. She couldn't believe I actually came over, but she was glad I did.

***

From Annette

Like Derek, I too was raised with God and faith at the forefront of my life. Derek was brought up as a Catholic, however, whereas I was brought up as a Southern Baptist. My dad was a minister, so I was the preacher's kid, otherwise known as the PK.

There are many misconceptions about being a Southern Baptist, as well as about being a PK. We were an ordinary family, though, even if having a dad who was a minister meant we didn't have an "ordinary" life. We had a good life. My dad didn't enter the ministry for the money. He entered it for the love of God and the people he served.

From the time I was born to the time I graduated from college, we moved six times. All the moves were within the state of North Carolina. We trekked the entire state from near the coast to the mountains. During our first year in the mountains, it snowed and snowed and snowed. I loved every minute of it. I remember getting out of school before Christmas because of the snow and not going back until the end of January. Of course, we paid for all those vacation days when we attended school until the end of June.

We were always a happy family, but when I was in the second grade my sister, who was about eighteen at the time, began to have difficulty walking. Debbie's gait became unsteady and was slowly getting worse. My parents enlisted the help of local doctors, but they were unable to provide a diagnosis. My parents then took Debbie to the North Carolina Baptist Hospital where her illness was finally diagnosed. A rare disease called Friedreich's ataxia, which only affects one out of every 50,000 people in the United States, was taking over her body. The prognosis wasn't good. Eventually, my sister would lose her ability to walk, talk, eat, and care for herself. All she would be left with was her mind, which would remain alert and intact. Her life expectancy was a mere twenty-eight years.

After that we moved again, only to have another life-altering event take place. After two years away at college, my brother came home for good. Frightening symptoms began to appear in Barry just like those seen in Debbie. My parents took him to Debbie's doctors, who confirmed our family's worst nightmare. Barry also had Friedreich's ataxia.

Two out of the three children in our family were already diagnosed with this rare, debilitating, and fatal disease, and I had not reached the age of onset. At the time I didn't think about it, but I am sure my parents held their breath as I approached my late teen years.

For all the sickness we struggled through daily, we were still a close-knit and happy family. My parent's compassionate attitude, perseverance, and fortitude taught me a lot about dealing with others. When taking Debbie and Barry out in public, although the majority of people were empathic, there were those who lacked compassion and gave insensitive stares or made hurtful comments. The composure my parents displayed during these times taught me an invaluable lesson about empathy and respect. Mom and dad accepted the grace God gave them and put their children first, displaying unwavering love. I didn't know it then, but their example of faith, kindness, and unconditional love became the cornerstone in my life, especially after the birth of my son.

The first time I saw Derek I was standing outside at a pay phone talking to my mom. I noticed this nice-looking guy walking by, and I remarked to my mom: "Oh, there goes that good-looking guy from South Africa."

She laughed and said, "Annette, you think maybe you can find someone on this continent?"

Little did I know that the good-looking guy strolling across the campus would be the love of my life, but I'm sure my mom had an inkling.

***

Our first "real date" was on a Saturday evening. We decided that we would go to Mass, grab a bite to eat, and see a movie. I was a bit nervous, because Annette said she had never been to a Catholic church and didn't know much about the religion. It wasn't just our religions that were dissimilar. We were also from two separate continents, which added cultural differences to the mix of our relationship. As different as our backgrounds were, however, our faith and belief in the importance of family were the same.

One of the first things I noticed about Annette was her laid-back southern nature coupled with her knack to say what was on her mind. In contrast, there's probably not a laid-back bone in my body, as I am very motivated. Although I'm typically a straight shooter, I also tend to be reserved. As our bond became deeper, we discovered that our differences seemed to complement each other. We remained concerned, however, that our religious differences might become a problem.

We eventually talked about our religions and, although different in some ways, we found that we shared the same core beliefs. We knew that the faith-based backgrounds our families had instilled in us would prove beneficial in our journey together. I didn't want to let Annette go, and we didn't want our relationship to end because of religion. She told me to remain positive. We would cross that bridge when we got to it.

Our relationship flourished. We began to talk about marriage. The issue of religion became a moot point as Annette decided to convert to Catholicism. She has often said the choice was easy for her, because not only did she love me but she also loved the structure of the Church and the beauty of receiving the Eucharist.

Seven months after we met, I proposed to her. Eight months later, we were married in a small Catholic church. My family wasn't able to travel to the States for the wedding, so we decided to keep it simple.

It's amazing that despite all of our differences we were united. We were united because, although our faiths were different in practice, both Annette and I had been brought up with a strong belief in God, faith, and family. Such things transcend cultural differences. As it turned out, it was our faith that would get us through all the obstacles we would have to face together.

Chapter 2

Annette and I knew that we would eventually start a family. Eight years into our marriage and no children, however, stirs up questions from family and friends as to when "the time would be right." We dodge the question as often as we can. It isn't that we're trying to hold on to our carefree lifestyle, but that in the back of our minds we're worried about passing on the Friedreich's ataxia that so negatively changed the lives of Annette's brother and sister.

Although the doctors assure us the possibility is low, we are reminded each day that there is still that slim chance, as we watch her sister and brother's conditions deteriorate. Eventually we decide to go to the hospital where Annette's sister and brother were treated to receive genetic counseling.

The testing is extensive, but the results give good news. In order for our child to inherit the disease, we would both have to carry it. Finally, we are able to think about having a child without fear of a genetic disease.

It is October when we find out that we are really going to be parents. It's hard to explain our feelings of being blessed, grateful, excited, anxious, and nervous, which are all rolled into one big emotion. We share the remarkable news with our families, and the excitement begins to flow. Finally, those inquiries would receive an answer! The popular response after hearing our exciting news: "You have no idea how your life is going to change!"

We were going to find out. It was definitely God's timing. He knew now was the right time for us. We had our entire family surrounding us, and we were going to need them.

Chapter 3

It is January 3, 1994, and there is nothing but excitement in the room. I watch the technician initiate our first sonogram. We talk about the Christmas just celebrated and how happy our families are in anticipating our new arrival. Suddenly the small talk ceases. The technician pauses. She looks closer at the monitor.

So we ask, "Is everything OK?"

The technician keeps her eyes on the monitor: "I'm sorry, I'm not allowed to discuss the sonogram. A report will be sent to your doctor, and he'll be in touch."

The thrill of the moment slips away, and fear enters. We leave the hospital wondering what might be wrong.

It isn't until lunch time the next day that we get the news. I have an urge to go visit Annette. I can't explain it. It just feels like she needs me. As soon as I exit the elevator, I hear hysterical sobs. The closer I get to Annette's office the louder her crying becomes. I reach the door and freeze. Her body is slouched over in a chair, her head rests in her hands, and her body is shaking uncontrollably. Her friend Margaret stands by her side and tries to console her.

So I ask, "What's wrong?"

Annette throws herself into my arms at the sound of my voice. She buries her head in my chest. Slowly she looks up, tears streaming down her cheeks: "Dr. Donner just called. He said something's wrong with the baby's heart. The baby will need a pacemaker at birth."

I was shocked by the way we'd gotten the news, over the phone while Annette was alone at work. We were totally caught off guard, not prepared like we would have been if we were in the hospital or the doctor's office. The doctor couldn't give us an official diagnosis but did refer us to a specialist.

Until we were able to talk to the specialist we'd be in the dark, not knowing what was wrong or how to care for our child.

It's amazing how, when faced with adversity, the human mind kicks into overdrive and reinstates some form of sanity. We begin to rationalize: *Maybe the technician made a mistake. Besides, the doctor would have called us into his office if it were serious. Maybe we're just overreacting.* Until we know for sure, our emotions fluctuate from worst-case to best-case scenarios.

When we do finally meet with the specialist, Dr. Vega, we aren't sure what to expect. He enters the exam room in green scrubs and a white jacket. He isn't alone. An entire crew of residents, clad in the same scrubs and jackets, follow him in. Suddenly, I feel like Annette and our unborn child are on display. I grab her hand and squeeze it tightly.

Introductions are brief. Just minutes later the scan begins. Dr. Vega studies the screen, pointing to various areas as the residents lean in to also examine the screen. This continues for some time until he finally turns his gaze on us: "Did Dr. Donner explain your baby's situation?"

"He told my wife something was wrong with the baby's heart," I respond quickly, "and a pacemaker would probably be needed."

He clears his throat before adding: "It's very serious. There is no positive news to give you. Your baby has a rare condition called hypoplastic left heart syndrome. The left side of your baby's heart is dead." He pauses, and then says, "The baby is fine in the womb, but once born he or she will die."

Did he just say die? *What happened to the pacemaker?*

"A pacemaker won't help," Dr. Vega continues. "The only way your baby will survive is with a heart transplant, and even that is a long shot."

My mind reels. The only life our baby is going to have is in the womb....

After that, Dr. Vega introduces Annette and me to Dr. Penski from pediatric cardiology and we follow him to his office. We sit across the desk from the doctor in a state of shock. I keep looking at Annette. Weeks before she glowed with happiness. I can't help but wonder how she will endure this ordeal. The maternal bond is already there.

I think about the surprise baby shower the ladies at her office have planned. This celebration of a new beginning will have be canceled. We'll have to stop decorating the nursery. The house will stay the same. There will be no reminders of what could have been.

Annette and I had gone through all kinds of genetic testing to be sure we weren't carriers of the illness her brother and sister had. We tried to plan, to give our child the best life we could, but something totally different happened. The heart, the most vital of parts, had not formed properly. How could we have planned for this? How will we endure it?

Side by side, hand in hand, Annette and I listen. We nod to acknowledge the doctor's words, but the news really isn't sinking in.

"Is there any hope for survival?" I finally ask.

The doctor shakes his head. "This condition is almost always fatal," he explains. "Without a sonogram this disease can go undetected. At birth, a hypoplastic baby looks no different from any other. Many times mother and baby are released from the hospital. A few days later the baby dies at home because the hole allowing blood flow closes up. We will do everything we can, but…"

Annette starts to cry. I am emotional too, but I try to stay strong for her.

"It's still early enough in the pregnancy," he adds. "You are within your rights to have an abortion."

Annette collects herself. Her words reassure me and ignite hope: "Abortion is not an option. If my child only has nine months to live, then it will be a happy nine months. We will let God decide his or her fate."

Annette's decision leaves no room for argument, but there is still a definite struggle going on between our faith and medical opinion. The doctors are making their recommendations and determining the outcome of our child's life based on the evidence before them. Naturally, their words will linger in our minds, but our faith asks us to think outside those boundaries. "All things are possible for God" (Mark 10:27), even if that's not a factor in the doctor's diagnosis.

We choose faith, not fate. Annette's words set the precedent for our family moving forward, and we move forward knowing the consequences. Our child will live in the womb without a problem, but once born there would be no guarantees. The odds were not in our favor, but we would still give our child that chance and Annette would carry the pregnancy to term.

Our faith proclaims the sanctity of life. That teaching, along with faith, grace, and prayer, would be the cornerstone of our foundation during this time.

Who were we to determine our child's destiny? That power wasn't in our hands—it belongs to God—and we were going to place our trust in him. After that, sticking to our decision would be easy.

The rest of the journey will be filled with obstacles. We know none of that will be easy, and just like today, every other day will be filled with emotions. Today, though, we rally and stand firm in our trust in God and the prayers going out to him for us.

Chapter 4

There have been many times in my life when the full comprehension of a situation has escaped me, but no situation has thrown me so much as the news of my child's diagnosis.

Annette and I decide to get a second opinion. We choose to go to the University of North Carolina's teaching hospital because of its cutting-edge technology and the fact that it's close to home. Although Annette and I know we have to do this, hesitation sets in as we stand in front of the entrance. I clutch Annette's hand tighter; despite everything going on she radiates a maternal glow. She is still strong, even while carrying a child with an uncertain future. It is in moments like these that my wife continues to amaze me. I truly believe God planned for us to be together in this moment, the greatest hurdle we have ever had to overcome.

Walking the UNC hospital hallways, everything looks the same. As we enter the doctor's office, I sign in and we wait to be called. Time passes at a snail's pace until we finally enter an exam room, similar to all the ones we've been in before. We know the procedure. Annette lays on the table, I sit by her side, and together we wait.

As we wait, my mind plays through the scenario I desperately want: *Annette and I watch the UNC-Chapel Hill doctor complete the ultrasound. A smile eases across his face as he informs us that the scan shows no abnormalities. The original diagnosis has been a mistake.*

This scenario ceases in my mind as the doctor enters. He introduces himself and then immediately commences the scan. I wait and watch for that smile I had imagined, but it never comes. Instead, his words are exactly those we've heard before. Two doctors from high-caliber hospitals have given us the same verdict. Reality starts to settle in. The cloud of gloom seems destined to hover above us.

In the days following this visit, a million questions race through my mind, but the two that keep repeating are *"How?"* and *"Why?"* I see Annette doing the same thing, constantly questioning herself: *"Maybe I'm to blame? Maybe I shouldn't have taken that Tylenol....Maybe I shouldn't have had that cough drop...."* I tell her that nothing she did caused this, but my words do not ease her mind. Nothing will do that.

It seems everywhere I turn I am confronted with visions of happy families with a healthy baby: on the television, at the mall, in the grocery store, even at church. Annette notices it too. This was supposed to be a happy time for us, the key word being *supposed*.

After Mass one Saturday night, we decided to speak to our parish priest, Father Joe. We explain the news about our baby.

In his heavy Irish brogue he replies, "Leave your worries at the altar. Let God help you through." He takes Annette's hand in his. "Let the light shine in. Wherever you are, open the curtains, raise the blinds, and get plenty of sunlight. Light is good for the soul and for healing."

After that things seem to change. Our families and friends unite around us, building a fortress of support. The more we share the diagnosis with friends and acquaintances, the more "lighted" our path becomes. Through their love, prayers, and encouragement our burden feels lighter.

Hope begins to spark.

Chapter 5

From Annette

My car hugs the curves of the two-lane road as I drive to another checkup. A few months have passed since the news of our child's condition, and while I try to stay positive, time hasn't made things better. How can it, as I watch my stomach grow and know my baby is safe now but will only have three more months of safety until uncertainty hits? I try not to think about the due date. I'm frightened that it may be the end. I try to remain positive, but today I let tears stream down my face and turn up the radio in the car.

Suddenly, a song comes on that changes my entire demeanor. I listen to the words that seem to speak to me. I rub my stomach. "This is our song," I tell my child. Then I sing as loud as I can:

> *I can see clearly now the rain is gone.*
> *I can see all obstacles in my way.*
> *Gone are the dark clouds that had me blind.*
> *It's gonna be a bright (bright)*
> *bright (bright) sunshiny day.*

["I Can See Clearly Now," Jimmy Cliff lyrics, 1993]

It's hard to explain, but I know this is a sign that we will persevere.

I've been a little apprehensive toward my current doctor. Trips to the office have not been an uplifting experience, but today I try to hold on to the good vibrations from the song.

The receptionist calls me over and says, "I want to let you know that Dr. Donner is in emergency surgery. Dr. Keever will see you today."

"That's fine," I respond. I think about seeing a new doctor. I've seen Dr. Keever at church, but that's about all I know of him.

I'm finally called to the exam room. Once there I am alone, which is a rarity these days, and the solitude gives me time to think. I have always been strong in my faith, relying on God in all aspects of my life. It is the foundation on which Derek and I have built our family life. It is very easy to live by faith when times are good, but troubling times put that foundation to the test. This is our test, our cross. I have choices: I can do nothing and hope everything goes OK, resign myself to the situation, or take control of it the best I can. I think about my faith and the prayers of family and friends. I know all these things fused together will sustain us. I think about the song on the radio and how it came on at the right moment.

My mom always says, "No one knows what tomorrow holds, but we know who holds it." No doctor or medical opinion can dictate the future of my child. Only the one above has control of the situation, and I need to place my trust in him. My job is to continue to pray, continue to ask others for their prayers, and make sure the remainder of my pregnancy is healthy and positive. Fear must be turned into perseverance.

Dr. Keever enters the room, tall, lanky, and full of life. "Hello, Miss Annette," he says in a slow, southern Alabama drawl.

"Hello," I answer. It seems odd knowing him from church and now seeing him in this capacity, but his demeanor has a settling effect.

"So, how are things going?" He takes a seat on the rolling stool and glances at my chart.

"Fine," I reply. That's the traditional Southern response to the question, no matter what the actually ailment or state of mind.

"Now, I know there is a lot going on in your life. Are you sure you are really fine?"

I smile, "Trying to be."

He signals for the nurse to enter and conducts the routine exam. Then he does something out of the ordinary and talks with me, not just about my feelings and apprehensions but about the possible outcome of my pregnancy. He is not bleak or pessimistic. He offers hope and encouragement.

"I always think it helps to hear about others who have overcome obstacles. Theirs may not be the same, but similar." He pauses before continuing: "You've made your decision to deliver this baby, and I applaud you. Remember to cherish the time you have with your child, whether it be a day, five years, or fifty years. Every day is a blessing. Stay positive!"

Before I leave, I inform the receptionist that I want Dr. Keever to be my physician from now on. He's the first doctor who didn't question our decision to carry the baby to term, and he reminded me there is always hope. I need to surround my baby and myself with positive reinforcements. Dr. Keever is one of them.

Chapter 6

From Annette

It's two in the morning, and I am tossing and turning. I slowly get out of bed, trying not to wake Derek, and go into the family room to turn on the television. I cannot get comfortable. No matter what I do, whether I sit, stand, or lay, I feel uneasy. I pace the floor most of the night. Finally, after four hours of restlessness, I go to the bathroom and my water breaks. I am in shock. This is it!

"Derek!" I call.

At the sound of my voice his feet hit the floor, and he is at the bathroom door in two seconds flat.

"I think it's time!" I say urgently. "Can you call my mom?"

My family lives next door, so my mom is by my side in minutes. I watch Derek and my mom whirl around each other like two mini tornadoes, trying to gather my things. My mom kneels beside me; she knows how anxious I am.

"Everything will be fine," she tells me with great conviction, and I believe her. She is my rock.

Once in the car everything seems surreal. Is this it? Is it really time? What is going to happen now? I pray: *Dear God, help me, help Derek, but most importantly help our baby.*

Derek helps me into the hospital. Within minutes, I am in a wheelchair on the way to my room. Derek and I toured the maternity floor early in my pregnancy, but I didn't remember the rooms being as large as mine. It doesn't feel like a hospital room; it is more comforting. Everything is decorated in light wood with pink wallpaper, which makes me wonder if they know something I don't.

Nurses come in and out. One nurse remains by my side making sure

19

I am comfortable. She tells me that she will be with me at all times and to let her know if I need anything. I don't know what I need. I do not know what I am supposed to be feeling. One thing I do know is that the pain is starting to intensify.

"How much longer?" I ask my nurse.

"Depends," she responds. "First-time deliveries can be long and drawn out. The doctor should be in soon."

Derek tries his best to make me comfortable, but *petrified* is the only word that describes how I feel. My baby is ready to enter this world, and after that it's up to God. Everyone is here except my mom who is at home caring for my brother and sister, but she has already started manning the phone, calling friends and family to start the prayer chain.

Over four hours after I arrive, there is a knock on the door and the doctor enters. I have never met him before. He walks in and introduces himself, shaking Derek's hand.

"Wow, you look just like Billy Crystal," Derek says.

Derek knows how to break the tension. I'm not sure if the doctor takes his remark as a compliment or not, but the resemblance makes me laugh. That will be the last time I laugh for a long time.

I've watched shows about moms giving birth and it always seems painful, but I can honestly say I do not feel the pain. All I feel is Derek's presence helping me.

At 1:27 in the afternoon, I hear the first cry of our baby.

"It's a boy!" the doctor says lifting him up for me to see.

I can't believe it. I'm not sure what I was expecting, but he is crying just like any normal baby. He is beautiful. He looks complete, ten fingers and ten toes, but we know he is incomplete. I only see him for an instant; there is no time to bond as he is whisked away. The joy of the moment goes out the door with him. I feel diminished. For nine months he has been a part of me. I have championed his cause, stayed positive, and prayed, and now I am unable to touch or feel his warmth.

I push Derek's hand, "Go see what's happening."

Because of the early diagnosis, the hospital is prepared for the arrival. All necessary precautions are being taken. Their job is to stabilize him and transport him to the North Carolina hospital, which awaits our son.

Chapter 7

Most parents have the joy of pondering over baby names as the day of their child's birth approaches, but Annette and I spent our time focusing on how he would survive and hadn't given names much thought. It was by the grace of God that my father suggested the name John Paul, after the Pope. Who better to name our son after than this strong, loving, and dedicated man? So, at 2:40 in the afternoon, John Paul George arrives at the neonatal intensive care unit (NICU) and is placed in a warm, waiting crib.

I am now torn between two hospitals: the one where my wife is recovering and the one my son is in. I stay with John Paul, but I am not prepared for the NICU. This is not like the movies. Tiny cribs line the walls, but these are overpowered by huge machines. Infants lay fighting for their lives. I head straight for the nurses' station and inquire about John Paul. The nurse there tells me to put on a surgical gown and follow her.

My heart pangs at the sight of him; he is beautiful yet vulnerable. He is swaddled in a white blanket with pink and blue stripes around the top. All that is visible is his face and his head full of coal-colored hair. At an inch closer to the side of his crib, I see that his nose is perfect and his lips are full and pink. He is sleeping, so I'm not sure about the color of his eyes, but his lashes are long. I can't believe my son is here. I pinch myself to confirm that I am not in a dream. I stand and watch his breathing; his chest heaves and relaxes.

Maybe there is nothing wrong with him, I think. Then I notice the color of his skin. It is not rosy pink like most babies but dusky gray. Every limb has some sort of apparatus attached, connecting him to monitors and machines. I am afraid to touch him. I stand there and stare.

A doctor approaches and introduces herself as Dr. Karen Renar. She talks about an echocardiogram performed earlier. The findings verify the diagnosis of hypoplastic left heart syndrome. Although I have known the diagnosis for nine months, her words confirming it have made it real and inescapable. She carefully discusses the options for management. The information overwhelms me. Approval must be given before a procedure can take place. Life and death decisions are starting already, and I must make them instantly.

At this point, she tells me that John Paul will need to be tube fed and intubated (placed on a respirator) and asks if I will consent. Terms I have never heard before are thrown at me. All I know is if it will help save my son's life, then I want it done.

I want John Paul baptized immediately and I request a priest, but I'm worried that he won't be able to come right away. I'm worried about what might happen to John Paul. I get a cup of water from the nurses' station. I know it isn't holy, but I know that Jesus will bless it and my son anyway. I pray silently by John Paul's side and dip my thumb into the water, making the sign of the cross on his forehead, in the name of the Father, the Son, and the Holy Spirit. My eyes moisten at this moment I'm able to share with my son. For that instant, life is still and I am at peace.

Chapter 8

The morning after his birth, my parents and I go to see John Paul during visiting hours. As I enter, my stomach churns. John Paul is intubated. He lays flat on his back, his arms and legs sprawled apart. When the doctor told me that they may have to intubate him, I really did not know what that meant, only that it would help him breathe. A large plastic blue tube protrudes out of his mouth. The tube connects to a ventilator. The noise from the ventilator reminds me of being in a wind tunnel. Next I notice a tube coming out of his nose. Part of the tube is taped to his cheek. My eyes follow the tube and find it hooked to a small machine on a chrome pole. A bag hangs from the top of the pole, and cream-colored liquid flows through the tube.

"What's that?" I ask the nurse.

"That is John Paul's food. He is being tube fed in order to receive nutrition."

I wish I had been able to put an image to those incomprehensible medical terms. I wish I had been prepared for how these images would make me feel. If I'd been told what to expect, maybe it would have reduced some of the anxiety.

My mom, dad, and I stand by John Paul. Not much is said, but we offer up prayers in the silence of our hearts. Our thoughts are interrupted by a doctor who introduces himself as Dr. Bland. I notice the accent right away, South African. I can't believe it, Dr. Bland is from my homeland! The kinship briefly eases my tension. He explains the options for John Paul, stating that a surgical procedure may help.

Never once in all those doctor visits has surgery ever been mentioned. We thought our only options were to do nothing or hope for a heart transplant. But now, surgery is an option. I can't believe it. Annette and I had agreed before that if surgery was an option to help our son, we would move forward with it.

"I'll set up an appointment for tomorrow, June 6, at 2 o'clock," Dr. Bland told us. "You will meet with Dr. Harmon, chief of cardiothoracic surgery. Dr. Penski and I will also be in attendance. Dr. Harmon will be able to answer any questions you may have about this option for John Paul."

My adrenaline is pumping. I can't wait to get back to the hospital and tell Annette there may be a surgical procedure to help John Paul.

Finally, there is tangible hope.

Chapter 9

I've been repeating the words Dr. Bland said to me at the hospital: "There may be a surgical procedure to help John Paul."

It is a wonderful possibility, but the more I think about it the more anxious I become. What will surgery entail? What will the outcome be? Dr. Bland did not give us any details, so Annette and I will have to wait twenty-four hours to find out; that means twenty-four hours to contemplate the unknown. I sit at the foot of Annette's hospital bed in deep conversation. We realize the importance of the meeting tomorrow with the surgeon; time is of the essence and a decision will have to be made promptly. In my heart I know what Annette and I want, but this isn't just about our wants anymore. We have to determine what is best for our son. The discussion is interrupted by a gentle knock on the door.

"Come in," I say, turning to face the door.

A priest enters. I believe God sends people into our lives for a reason, and he sent this priest to us at the exact moment we needed him. After a few minutes of small talk, we begin to tell the priest of John Paul's situation and our dilemma.

"You've done your part. You've brought John Paul into the world. Now let John Paul show you what he can do."

With these words, we receive our counsel. We know what we need to do.

When Annette is finally released, we go to the hospital so she will have an opportunity to see John Paul and know that he is alive and exists before we begin the road toward surgery.

"It's important for you to hold John Paul and bond with him," I tell her as we walk down the hall of the hospital. "Dr. Bland encouraged me to make sure you do that." She doesn't respond; she hasn't said much since we got out of the car.

"Are you OK?"

She shakes her head and tries to smile, but I can sense the worry. I cannot fathom what she feels, both emotionally and physically. I would not push the bonding issue, but Dr. Bland has been insistent about its importance, so I try and convey this to Annette.

We both pause at the entrance of the NICU. I take her hand. I've tried to prepare her for what she is about to see. Her grip tightens. I open the door, and we walk hand in hand. I watch her eyes scan from one crib to the next.

"This is so sad, look at all these babies." Her eyes fill with fear, as she adds, "I don't know if I can handle this."

I gently tug her hand and pull her to John Paul's crib. She walks over and stands beside him. Her trembling hand caresses his face. Her eyes lock with mine, "He's beautiful." Tears stream down her face. I place my arm tightly around her.

"Would you like to hold him?" the nurse asks.

Her eyes remain on John Paul. "There're so many tubes and everything."

"Honey, that's no problem."

Annette hesitates, "Maybe tomorrow."

The nurse explains all the tubes and machines to Annette, who tries to focus on the words, but her attention is consumed by our son. After the nurse leaves, we stand by the bed together, one of us on each side of John Paul.

I glance at Annette and again ask, "Are you OK?"

"This is overwhelming, all the machines and everything. I know you tried to prepare me, but seeing John Paul in this condition is just…." She stops short of finishing the sentence. I notice her bottom lip quivering. Unable to contain herself any longer she breaks down in my arms. Months of anxiety and pressure are released. Annette then pulls away, wipes her eyes, and moves closer to John Paul. The tips of her fingers stroke his hair.

"Do you think he can hear us?" she asks me.

"I know he feels our presence, and yes, I think he can hear us. That's why it's very important we talk to him, touch him, kiss him, tell him we love him, and make sure he feels our love."

The nurse interrupts our conversation to inform us that the surgeon is waiting in the conference room down the hall. I squeeze John Paul's hand, and Annette kisses him on the forehead before we leave.

Outside of the NICU we pause.

"Isn't it amazing? That's our son in there," Annette says beaming.

"Are you sure you didn't want to hold him?" I ask her.

"No. It seems everyone is pushing the subject of bonding, and it makes me uncomfortable. It's like the doctors and nurses want me to bond because they do not expect John Paul to live and our bonding needs to take place before it's too late." She stops in the hallway and looks directly into my eyes, "I don't know, maybe I'm just scared."

When we finally enter the conference room we see Dr. Penski and Dr. Bland. The surgeon introduces himself as we enter.

"Hello, I am Dr. Harmon, chief of cardiothoracic surgery."

We introduce ourselves and sit across the table from the doctor.

Dr. Harmon, who is very personable, in his mid-fifties, with fair hair and blue eyes, begins the conversation with optimistic news: "I examined your son and he is a good candidate for the Norwood procedure."

I look at Annette and then back to Dr. Harmon. "What is the Norwood procedure?"

The doctor explains the very complicated medical procedure in a way that's simple enough for Annette and me to understand. The goal of this procedure is to have the right side of the heart, which normally only pumps blood to the lungs, pump blood to the entire body. The Norwood procedure is split into three different stages. The first stage, conducted a few days after birth, allows the right side of the heart to pump blood to the upper body. This stage determines if the heart is strong enough to withstand the pressure of what it is being asked to do. The second stage reroutes the blood to the midsection of the body. This stage usually takes place during the first year after birth. The third and final stage takes the blood to the lower extremities and completes the three-stage procedure. This stage is usually completed when the child is about three years of age. The Norwood procedure is entirely experimental, as Dr. Harmon makes crystal clear to me and Annette. Although Dr. Harmon has performed the Norwood procedure before, the surgery has never been attempted at the North Carolina hospital.

"I'll be perfectly honest, the odds are not good." Dr. Harmon leans across the table and shows a diagram of the heart. "One thing in John Paul's favor, the hole that allows blood flow is larger than normal. Therefore, he is better suited for this surgery."

Questions go back and forth. I try to soak up everything the doctor says. This goes on for over an hour and a half; finally the doctors leave me and Annette alone in the conference room to contemplate all the information tossed at us. There is so much to process, but time is short. We must make our decision by morning.

With the profound words of the priest still fresh in our minds, we make our decision and go back to the NICU to visit John Paul. We find Dr. Harmon at John Paul's bedside.

"He's a lovely child," Dr. Harmon says.

"Thank you," Annette responds. She walks over and stands beside the doctor.

"We made our decision. We have done our part. Now let John Paul show us what he can do."

Dr. Harmon nods.

Annette tugs at the doctor's arm. "Please take good care of him."

Chapter 10

Today is excruciating. Annette and I stand by John Paul's crib. It is almost more than I can stand.

Every part of my body trembles. I can't control it. This is the most important day of his young life, and I am fearful it may be the last time I see him alive. I shouldn't be thinking this way, but I can't help it. The consent forms have been signed. Everything is in black and white, and complications from the surgery include death. John Paul has only been in my life for five days, but his impact has been astronomical. I can't tolerate the thought of losing him, and I know Annette feels the same.

"This is tough," she says, her words soft, almost a whisper. "He's going to be fine," she adds, but her eyes ask it as a question.

I respond with conviction, "Absolutely. He's going to be fine." Even though I have doubts, I have to believe my own words. Nothing else in the world matters right now.

Only two family members are allowed in the NICU at a time, but today the rules are bent for us. The nurse allows both of our parents to stay with us until John Paul leaves for surgery. We gather around his crib, talk to him, tell him we love him, and to be strong because Jesus is with him. I feel a slight touch on my back. I turn and notice a nun in a cream-colored habit.

"I'm Sister Eileen Dennis from St. Paul's," she explains.

"It's a pleasure to meet you, Sister. My name is Derek, and this is my wife Annette." I introduce our parents. She enters the circle we have formed around John Paul.

"What a beautiful boy. What's his name?"

"His name is John Paul. We named him after the pope."

"That's lovely." She steps closer to John Paul. Her wrinkled hand slowly touches his head. She leans down and whispers something in his ear. She stands by his side for a few minutes, her hand clasped around his arm, her eyes focused intently on my son.

"Who is John Paul's doctor?" she asks, returning to my side.

"Dr. Harmon."

"He's a great doctor and a good Christian man. I have known him for a long time."

She must see the worry in my eyes, because she gathers Annette and me closer to her and takes both of our hands into hers.

"Is John Paul your only child?"

"Yes, Sister," we respond in unison.

"Ask Jesus to place John Paul's heart in his Sacred Heart and to place the surgeon's hands in his hands."

Talk about a godsend. This pint-sized lady is a full-sized blessing, a person God has sent into our lives for a reason.

As the surgical team arrives to take John Paul to surgery the mood becomes somber. Sister Dennis excuses herself and tells us she will see us later. Our parents each kiss John Paul and go to the waiting room. Annette and I remain. We watch the team dressed in green scrubs prepare to move John Paul. The nurse approaches, "If you like, you may walk down to the OR with John Paul."

"We'd like that, thank you."

We follow our son down the corridor to a special elevator. Inside the elevator, I notice my legs are like strings of spaghetti. I back up against the wall to steady myself. The doors open. Annette and I follow John Paul down a short hallway. Ahead I see the entrance to the operating room. I begin to wonder if I will be able to keep my composure.

"This is as far as you can go," the surgical team tells us as they prepare to bring John Paul into the room.

I lean down, make the sign of the cross on John Paul's forehead, and repeat Sister Dennis' words, "Please, sweet Jesus, I place John Paul's heart in your Sacred Heart. Please place the surgeon's hands in your sacred hands." I slowly kiss him and soak up his sweet newborn scent. I stand back, and Annette places her index finger inside John Paul's hand. I watch his grip tighten around his mother's finger. Tears well up in my eyes. Annette leans in and kisses his cheek. Reluctantly we step away and watch him enter the operating room. Our eyes follow him until he is no longer visible. Annette and I slowly walk down the hallway in silence. We are both too overwhelmed to speak.

We wait in the surgical waiting room on the first floor of the hospital. The large windowless room is lined with chairs, vending machines, and an information desk staffed with volunteers. Annette and I find our families and begin our long wait. The clock on the wall moves slower with every passing hour. I walk to the information desk for a status update each hour, but the answer is the same, still in surgery. I do not know what to do with myself. Finally, after ten hours a volunteer calls over the speaker, "George family." Annette and I rush to her desk.

"John Paul George is out of surgery."

"Is he OK?" I ask.

"I'm sorry, that's all the information I have. The doctor will be in shortly."

A heavy weight lifts off my shoulders. At least John Paul is out of surgery, but doubt trickles in. *Sure, he's out of surgery, but what if....* I think back to the day Annette had the sonogram and having to wait on the doctor for results. I know I am being paranoid. I shake my head to clear my thoughts. Annette puts her arms around my waist and squeezes tightly.

We walk back, tell our family the news, and sit in momentary relief.

Annette jolts out of her chair, "There's Dr. Harmon."

I stand up beside her, frozen, unable to move. Dr. Harmon is still wearing his surgical cap, and his mask is loosely draped around his neck. I try to analyze his face as he walks toward us. He meets us with a weak smile.

"The surgery went well. John Paul is in recovery."

Before I know it, Annette is hugging Dr. Harmon and thanking him profusely. I do the manly thing, a firm handshake, but as emotions soar I end up hugging him as well. He doesn't seem to mind. In his eyes I see the same thankfulness that we are feeling.

"The next forty-eight hours will be crucial. He should be up in 5A, which is the intensive care unit, in an hour and a half. Go get something to eat, and I will see you up there later."

"Thank you, doctor. Thank you so much."

Annette repeats the same words. We do not know what to do with ourselves and are ecstatic. We share the news with our family and count our blessings. One hurdle cleared! Finally, I am able to breathe. I exhale and resolve myself to focusing on John Paul's recovery.

"Let's go to the cafeteria and get something to eat," Annette says, tugging at my arm. I can't remember the last time Annette and I had something to eat, and with this good news we finally feel able to focus on those needs.

Since John Paul's birth, Annette has been too stressed to eat a real meal, so it's with delight that I watch her devour a cheeseburger and French fries. We do not want to waste much time. As soon as we eat, Annette and I go up to the fifth floor and wait in the small ICU waiting area. As the day turns to evening, I find myself ending where I started, waiting. Finally, the nurse calls us to the ICU.

The ICU on the fifth floor is for adult heart patients. It is very rare for a newborn to be in the unit. Annette and I enter. The unit is full, and the sound of machines stationed by each bed is intense. From the doorway, I see John Paul's crib in the middle of the floor directly in front of the nurses' station. I notice the same machines from the NICU surround him, but as I inch closer my heart drops. Nothing could have prepared me for the image now before me.

Dear God. Is this the same baby?

If it wasn't for his hair, I would not have recognized my son. It is difficult for me to describe the sight. His face is like a balloon, his eyes are swollen shut, just the tips of his long lashes are visible, and his skin is black and blue. In the middle of John Paul's tiny chest is an incision smothered with Betadine solution; it stretches the length of his chest. At this moment, I realize that this incision will turn into a scar, a scar that will be a daily reminder of my son's plight. How will I explain the scar to him when the time comes?

Visiting hours ended long ago, but the doctors allow Annette and me to remain a few minutes longer with our son. We both stand beside the crib in disbelief, unsure what to do or how to act. Sister Dennis arrives and joins us. Together we silently pray for his recovery. The nurse in charge of John Paul gives Annette a sheet of paper with a visiting hours schedule and a phone number for her to call for updates. We are told that the unit strictly adheres to these scheduled times for the well-being of the patients.

It is time to go, but I can't bear to leave. We will not be allowed back in until ten o'clock the next morning. The nurse assures us she will call if there is any change. I kiss John Paul on the top of his head and start toward the door. It's a struggle. I look back repeatedly before I finally exit through the automatic doors.

A good night's sleep; I do not know what that is. Since the birth of John Paul, my sleep is restless because of too many constant worries. The worrying is exhausting, but I am still unable to sleep. Annette feels the same way. She calls the hospital throughout the night for updates.

Finally, a ray of sun pierces through the window and with it the hope of a new day. Annette and I arrive at the hospital early and wait for visiting hours to commence. Fifteen minutes is all the time allotted. We remain at the hospital throughout the day, waiting for the next fifteen minutes. At night, we make it home around nine o'clock and sleep intermittently between Annette's calls to the hospital for updates. After a couple of days, we just stop going home, choosing instead to stay at the hospital around the clock.

The doctors explained the complexity of the surgery during our conference, but in my naiveté I failed to consider the obstacles of recovery and aftercare. We've been through the first eight days of recovery and there have been some bumps, but nothing major. On June 16, the doctor says John Paul is ready to be extubated (meaning his breathing tube will be removed, being no longer necessary to sustain his life). I am excited. If the doctors feel he is ready to breathe on his own that is a major accomplishment.

John Paul has two hours without the tube before the complications set in and he has to be reintubated. The excitement of earlier begins to wane. It seems John Paul is on a downhill spiral.

By June 19, on my first Father's Day with John Paul, he takes a turn for the worse. His platelets and white blood cell count have decreased as has his blood sugar.

"I have contacted Dr. Shaw. There is a possibility that John Paul's bowel is dying," Dr. Harmon explains in response to the evaluation of John Paul's abdominal X-ray and abnormal blood work.

Dr. Harmon advises that an exploratory surgery is needed. If the bowel is dead, it will be removed.

Naturally, I am concerned. John Paul has just had open heart surgery and now this. "What if his heart is unable to withstand the pressure of a surgery?" I ask. Dr. Harmon assures me there is no other alternative. The surgery has to be done.

I sign the consent form, and within minutes Annette and I watch as John Paul is wheeled away again. Doctors and nurses surround his crib. The ventilator that breathes for him is still in the ICU, so a nurse must manually bag John Paul in place of the ventilator and with every step the others monitor his vitals.

My spirit sinks. *This can't be my first and last Father's Day rolled into one!*

Once again, Annette and I take our seats in the surgical waiting room. I notice that there is no volunteer stationed at the desk and the seats are plentiful this late on a Sunday afternoon. Mentally drained, all I have the strength to do is sit and tightly hold Annette's hand. Around six o'clock, I see Dr. Shaw walk into the waiting room. The news is good. John Paul's bowel is fine, and he is back in the ICU. Cultures from his central lines grew Escherichia coli and several other staph infections, but antibiotics have been started to try and clear these infections.

Back in the ICU, I stand by the crib and cannot help but notice where another scar will be. Right where his vertical incision from the open heart surgery ends begins the horizontal incision from the stomach surgery.

But these scars are superficial. I just thank God for blessing me this Father's Day with my beautiful son.

Chapter 11

The uncertainty continues. John Paul is going back in the operating room for adjustments to the first stage of the Norwood procedure. Dr. Harmon plans to modify the shunt between the pulmonary arteries and the aorta. This is necessary because John Paul has developed pulmonary hypertension. The tiny arteries in his lungs have become narrow or blocked, causing increased resistance to the flow of blood in the lungs and raising pressure within the pulmonary arteries. As the pressure builds, his heart's lower right chamber (right ventricle) must work harder to pump blood through his lungs. If not addressed, this will eventually cause the heart muscle to weaken and possibly fail completely. The consensus of the doctors: the shunt is too small and needs to be widened to allow proper blood flow. Again, Annette and I must wait.

My emotions bounce from place to place, and I can't get them to settle. Annette is no better than I am. In fact, I'm starting to get concerned about her state of mind. She hardly eats. The last time she had a full meal was June 9. Her current diet consists of coke, crackers, and a candy bar every now and then. Her face is hollow. I do not know how much more she can take.

Worry hangs over me constantly for my wife and my son. Even on days when everything seems to be running smoothly, there is that constant worry of what will go wrong next. I thought after the first surgery that John Paul was on the road to recovery. Then on Father's Day, there was the stomach surgery, then watching him struggle with a serious staph infection, and now the shunt.

Every day is a challenge to my faith, and I don't know when it will end.

35

From Annette

I am on autopilot, going through the motions as I wait for my son to recover. My son has had to clear so many hurdles, and I'm in awe of all the miracles John Paul has been blessed with in his short life. I am grateful that the doctors were able to revise his shunt and pray this is the last obstacle.

Derek and I stand by John Paul's crib where we have been since he returned from surgery. His vitals are good. We are overcome with relief. It's late. Dr. Renar encourages us to go home and get a good night's sleep. I am reluctant to leave John Paul's side, and I know Derek is too. Dr. Renar can see the stress on our faces, the weariness is starting to take over, and she insists we get some rest. She argues that it will be better for us to be refreshed when John Paul wakes up. Neither of us intends to leave, but Dr. Renar makes a logical point and eventually she persuades us to take a break. We kiss John Paul goodbye and, hesitatingly, depart.

As soon as we get home, I call the nurses' station to check in. With confirmation that John Paul is still doing fine, I finally go to bed. That peace doesn't last long. It's only midnight when the phone rings and we are summoned back to the hospital. John Paul has taken a turn for the worse. I've only been a mother for a short time, but I'm already wishing I'd listened to my maternal instincts and insisted we stay the night at the hospital.

Everything is a blur until I enter the ICU. Then everything before my eyes becomes vivid and crystal clear. John Paul is in dire straits. He has a team of doctors and nurses hovering over his crib, all of whom are wondering what tactic they need to take next. Dr. Renar approaches, anxiety etched on her face. My knees buckle. The news can't be good.

She explains that John Paul's saturations are dropping dangerously low, his brain and lungs are being starved for air, and the trauma places extreme pressure on his already frail heart. As a last resort, John Paul is going to be placed on a jet ventilator to try to revive his oxygen levels. She adds that the prognosis is not good and the chance of survival is very slim to none.

We don't want to leave, but Derek and I are asked to wait outside in the waiting room. I watch Derek make his way through the doctors and nurses until he is beside John Paul's crib. He leans down and whispers something into our son's ear, kisses him, and then together we exit intensive care and enter the waiting room.

Chapter 12

We are alone in the small room. Our hands are entwined, but we don't speak, both of us absorbed in our own thoughts. For no particular reason, my eyes are focused on the door and the bare hallway outside as I fervently pray for my son.

Out of nowhere, an elderly black man in his eighties appears at the door. I don't recognize him, which is unusual as we have gotten to know most of the employees from being at the hospital around the clock. He has one hand on a large gray trashcan he had been pulling, and the other hand is rubbing his knee.

"My knee is killing me. I need to take a seat for a few minutes," he says.

I don't take much notice of him. I keep my head bowed thinking of my son. The man comes in, sits in the empty chair next to me, and proceeds to rub both of his knees as he speaks.

"Family's real important." His voice is firm, yet soothing.

"Yes, I know," I say, not looking up.

He removes his right hand from his knee and places it on mine. As soon as his hand touches my leg a warm sensation radiates through me. I raise my head and stare at him. I am captivated by his eyes; they are brilliant blue, the color of the Caribbean Sea. His gaze offers serenity.

"My son, you have a child in there."

"Yes, but it doesn't look good."

With surety he says, "Don't worry, everything is going to be fine."

I think to myself, *who is this guy and why is he telling me this with such conviction?* But no sooner have I thought this than a nurse rushes into the waiting room.

"Hurry, come quick!"

Annette and I run out the door and follow her to the ICU expecting the worse. As I enter, Dr. Renar is standing in the middle of the room shaking her head, not in disgust, but rather with a smile on her face. When I see the smile I feel weightless.

"I can't understand this!" she exclaims.

I stand in disbelief. "What happened?"

"John Paul's saturations have shot back up and his functions are returning to normal. We did everything humanly possible to make this work, but this miracle could have only come from one place." Her eyes gaze upward, and her hands point toward heaven.

Divine intervention has acted for John Paul. I think of the elderly man with the Caribbean blue eyes who just told me everything was going to be OK. I have to find this man to tell him the good news. I make a mad dash out of the ICU and run down the hall to the waiting room. It is empty. I look in every room, but I can't find him.

Exhausted, I run back into the ICU and ask the nurses about the custodian who works the night shift. I give a detailed description of him, but they stand dumbfounded. They have never seen the gentleman I described. Custodians do not work in the middle of the night.

Bewildered, I slowly walk back over to John Paul. The warm sensation delivered by the man still remains. I reach down and place my index finger into John Paul's hand and think of the words spoken: "Don't worry, everything is going to be fine."

Angels wear many faces and can appear in the oddest places. In my wildest dreams, I never imagined a blue-eyed angel delivering hope and comfort in my darkest hour. I remain in awe at what happened.

Chapter 13

It has been nearly two months since John Paul ventured into the world. It goes without saying that his life thus far has been complicated, but he is not alone. I am sitting beside his crib in the NICU taking note of the surroundings. Our son is one of these small, helpless beings, hooked up to machines for a better chance at survival. We have watched other families' dark days. When their child has fought long enough, my heart cannot bear to see the pain. Then there are the joyful days, when we watch a child go home.

The NICU is its own world, and the world outside is a distant place. I can honestly say that for over fifty days nothing going on beyond the doors of the NICU matters to me. My only concern is my son, and today is our big day. I have been praying for this day. John Paul is coming home.

My excitement and anxiety mold into one. I am happy to take my son home, but that means we lose the security of having a doctor or nurse at our fingertips. Kathy, John Paul's nurse from the NICU, will be able to visit our home twice a week to help with any needs or concerns, so we will not be entirely on our own.

The last few days have been a crash course in home health care. Annette and I have both been retrained and certified in CPR. We have been shown how to administer his medications and insert his feeding tube. The feeding tube is without a doubt the most difficult. In order to receive nutrition, a small tube must be inserted into John Paul's nose. The tube is measured and then slowly pushed down into his stomach. Proper placement is vital. In the hospital, each insertion is checked by X-ray. At home, a stethoscope will be used to check placement.

Today is the test to verify if I am able to complete the insertion. Slowly, I insert the tube. I take the stethoscope and place it on John Paul's stomach.

With a syringe, I push air through the tube and listen for the specific sound that lets me know that the placement is correct. I nod my head to the nurse that the placement is correct; she verifies with a swish of air through the tube. She smiles, pats me on the back, and says, "Good job."

In order for John Paul to be released, both parents must be able to complete the insertion procedures. Annette is next. She is understandably nervous. Her hands tremble, but she carefully inserts the tube and continues the steps. "I think I got it!" she says with a smile, taking the stethoscope out of her ears. The nurse verifies this and congratulates her on a job well done.

Now that our son really will be coming home, Annette and I begin to take down all the religious statues, prayers, and medals that have adorned John Paul's crib at the hospital. Afterward, Kathy walks with me to the car and certifies that the car seat I purchased months ago is inserted correctly.

Next step: homeward bound.

It is the most wonderful feeling in the world walking through the front door with my son in my arms. I have longed for this day. I cannot believe it. My family is home, together, under one roof.

Chapter 14

I walk down the cold fluorescent-lit corridor of the hospital. In my arms is John Paul, now four months old. I open the door to the first-floor waiting room, and my body is numb with fear. This could be it, the last time I hold my son. Each time the nurse calls a patient, I hold my breath. Finally, she approaches. Her arms reach out. I instinctively tighten my grasp, but she pulls John Paul out of my arms. He screams, his eyes pleading with me, and it seems to me as if he is thinking, "W*hy are you letting her take me away? Save me!*" I will never forget that look. I hear his cry through the closed door, and it is all too much for me to take. I leave the room, walk into the hallway, and cry.

John Paul has come back for the second stage of the Norwood procedure. The second stage concentrates on blood flow to the middle part of the body. Of the three stages, it is the least complicated. Knowing this does not ease my anxiety. There are always complications associated with any surgery. Annette and I wait with our families in the same waiting room we did for the previous surgery. The scene is familiar; we know what to expect and realize the wait will be long. I find myself going through the same routine from months ago: praying and pacing. Repetition does not make the wait easier; if anything it is harder this time. Sister Dennis, who was such a comfort to us during our first stay, enters the waiting room and patiently waits with me and Annette. I look at the clock on the wall. My stomach begins to churn. John Paul has been in surgery longer than he was the last time. The worry takes over, my pacing increases, and my prayers become more fervent. Annette walks up to me, places her arms around my waist, and lays her head on my chest. Her body trembles. I squeeze her tightly, leading her over to two chairs where we sit hand in hand and continue our wait.

"George family." Finally, someone calls us over. "Dr. Harmon will be in shortly."

Minutes seem like hours, but at last I see Dr. Harmon enter the surgical waiting room. The smile on his face triggers a sigh of relief. Annette and I listen intently to the great news. The surgery has been successful, with no complications. John Paul is in recovery and will be in the PICU soon.

The PICU consists of one large room with beds stationed throughout. There are only two other children inside it. I remember what John Paul looked like after his first surgery, so I prepare for the worst. At first, all I see are machines, just like before, providing life to my son. I hold my breath and walk closer. When I finally see John Paul, I let out my breath in relief. He looks remarkably well compared to his first surgery. His skin is rosy, and although his face is swollen, it is not to the point where he is unrecognizable. I stand and look at him, Annette by my side. I am thrilled but still cautious. I remember the complications of the first surgery and the ups and downs Annette and I were forced to go through for two months. I try to block out those thoughts to focus on my son here in the present.

Two weeks later, we are able to take John Paul home. Any complications were minor. We are spared the roller coaster this time. Still, every time one hurdle is cleared I can't help but start thinking about the next one.

The third surgery is the final stage of the Norwood procedure. This stage routes blood to the lower part of the body and determines if half a heart can withstand the pressure of everything it is being asked to do. Knowing we still have this final stage to get through sits in the back of my mind constantly, but I try not to let it get in the way of the time I have with my son now. I try to take advantage of every minute. Every day is a precious gift.

Chapter 15

Decorations dangle from the ceiling, and balloons float throughout the house. I watch cars begin to pull up the driveway. John Paul is in top form with toys strewed everywhere. He sits in the middle of the foyer with his new friend, Bonkers, a bright orange, round toy with long, lime-green suction legs. When turned on, Bonkers goes berserk, bouncing around on his six skinny legs. The name fits. He drives me bonkers, but John Paul enjoys his craziness, so I sacrifice my sanity.

We are getting ready to celebrate John Paul's first birthday, and everyone who has been a part of and helped to sustain his life is invited. He does not realize the significance of this day, of course, but for me it is monumental. The doorbell rings and guests begin to arrive. John Paul stays in the middle of the foyer flashing a smile to those who enter. The decorated boxes and bags that collect on the couch spark his curiosity, as does the house now full of people.

I place John Paul in his high chair. His eyes scan all the people in front of him. He is unsure of what is happening. His bottom lip begins to quiver until he sees the cake with a candle and hears the people begin to sing.

"Happy birthday to you, happy birthday to you, happy birthday, John Paul, happy birthday to you."

A smile widens across his face. He claps his hands and kicks his feet. I place the cake in front of him, kiss him on the top of his head, and tell him to make a wish and blow out the candle.

He takes a deep breath and blows with all his might. The flame vanishes, the group surrounding John Paul cheers, and he smiles at his accomplishment. His index finger touches his lip. He is in deep thought. He eyes the cake, suddenly digs his hands into it, scoops it up in the palms of his hands, and shoves it into his mouth. Cake and icing plaster his face from his chin to the tip of his nose. Even his long lashes flutter with white and blue frosting. I stand back and let him enjoy the moment as I absorb every detail of this happy occasion.

Later that evening, I walk into John Paul's room, sit in the rocker, and watch him sleep. The moonlight cascades through the window, casting a subtle glow on my son. I think back to a year ago. The events of the past begin to replay in my mind. This journey is far from over.

Chapter 16

The period from November 1994 through July 1995 is indescribable. Thanksgiving and the first Christmas with my son is like no other I have ever experienced. The joy of Christmas is truly best when experienced through the eyes of a child. Our family celebrates the birth of Jesus with new eyes, sincerely thanking him for the miracles he's worked in John Paul's life. Every holiday seems to hold more meaning now that John Paul is with me, and it goes without saying that his first birthday was a great milestone.

This sense of contentment doesn't last. On August 15, John Paul goes to bed around seven o'clock and sleeps until he wakes up at five o'clock in the morning, crying uncontrollably. Annette and I both try to calm him, but nothing works. Annette phones the pediatrician who advises her to give John Paul some Tylenol and a warm bath. After the warm bath, John Paul vomits.

Annette and I have a hard time staying grounded when John Paul is ill. There are too many "what ifs" and complications for us to consider. Annette calls the pediatrician again, and this time we are instructed to take John Paul to the hospital.

John Paul screams in agony the entire trip. The emergency room is packed. John Paul's condition means he cannot wait, not to mention the danger of being around other illnesses as we wait with other patients to find out his current diagnosis. I rush to the nurse's desk and explain the situation. Luckily the nurse is understanding and places us in a room away from other patients. I lay John Paul on the table, and he squirms and cries with pain. I try cradling his legs to his stomach, but this does not help. A nurse takes his vitals and listens as Annette explains the situation.

John Paul is put under continuous observation for two days, but the doctors are still unable to determine a cause for the pain. John Paul is being fed intravenously and starts spitting up small amounts of yellowish green fluid before he begins to have the dry heaves. An X-ray of his abdomen shows a small bowel obstruction. Emergency surgery is scheduled. Dr. Shaw, the surgeon who operated on his bowel previously, will conduct the surgery. I am concerned about John Paul going through yet another surgery. The risks seem too high. I call my doctor friend John to get his opinion, but his wife answers. John is on his way to a medical conference and isn't there to take my call. Linda promises to try and get in touch with John when the plane lands at the airport. We should, hopefully, only have to wait a few minutes.

A doctor asks for a signature of consent, but I ask for more time. If we do this, I want to make sure it is because there are no other options. I pray for John's plane to be on time, for him to hear the page, and for him to call us back. Within thirty minutes the phone rings.

"You have no other choice," John says. "The source of the pain has to be determined." It isn't the hoped-for outcome, but now we feel more confident moving forward.

Annette signs the anesthesia consent form, and I sign the operation consent form. John Paul is rushed to surgery.

It is determined that scar tissue from the surgery last year is the cause of John Paul's pain and vomiting. Thankfully, there is nothing more serious wrong, and John Paul is discharged a few days later.

***

This episode brings home to us the fact that John Paul must be in near-perfect shape when he goes in for his third-stage surgery. The cold weather in North Carolina is a hindrance to John Paul's health. Fall and winter bring the cold and flu season. To keep John Paul healthy, we have to keep him indoors at all times. I want to be proactive, get him to a warmer climate, a place where he can play outside, enjoy the sunlight, and grow without worrying about what the environment or harsh weather might do to his health.

Growing up, I longed for independence to make my own decisions. Now, I wish someone could make this hard choice for me. In my heart, I know what I need to do for my son—move to a warmer climate. I dread the thought of leaving family and friends, and I know the move will be excruciating for Annette. She and her family are very close and have never been separated. I have an established business that I have nurtured for years in the area. By moving, we lose those securities.

From Annette

One of the hardest decisions I have ever faced is packing up to move to Florida. I will not miss the superficial things, the changing seasons, or the familiar rural beauty, but I am apprehensive to leave my family. During the beginning of John Paul's illness, many asked how I endured the stress and obstacles associated with a sick child. My response was always the same: God, faith, and the best role models, my parents. I have watched my parents give their total devotion to my brother and sister, doing whatever it took to make sure they received the best possible care. That is what Derek and I want for John Paul. We have to do what is best for our son in preparation for his third surgery. So, we make the decision to leave for Florida.

Derek's family decides to make the move to Florida with us, which offers some comfort, but it will not completely fill the void left by the absence of my own family. My spirit is broken. I choke back tears as we drive down the shadowy road. Daylight creeps up, and I am able to reclaim my perspective with the image of John Paul in the rearview mirror.

Chapter 17

The move has been tough, but I will endure anything for my son. Everything is new and different, yet the landscape reminds me of my home in South Africa. The warm weather is a great benefit to John Paul, who is able to go outside and play almost every day. The two of us are inseparable. He is always on my heels following me around the house and anywhere else I go.

Another thing I have noticed since moving to Florida is that John Paul has a natural talent for swinging the golf club. It is amazing how God works. Golf is not strenuous, so it is one of the few sports he will be able to actually do. I try to nurture his talent by taking him to the driving range and golf course on a regular basis. Still, even as we begin to settle into a routine, the question of when the next surgery will be constantly surfaces in my mind. Just before John Paul's third birthday, I receive the answer.

The cardiologist feels it is time. He is pleased with John Paul's progress and his growth. I am not sure I am ready for what lies ahead. Knowing the time is here causes many sleepless nights. The question that now plagues me is where to have the surgery performed.

The complications from the first stage haunt me. I do not know if the hospital in North Carolina is equipped to handle the serious third and final stage. William Imon Norwood, Jr., the doctor who invented the procedure, pioneered the surgery at Children's Hospital of Philadelphia, a hospital with an outstanding reputation. Annette and I seriously debate the pros and cons of taking John Paul to Philadelphia. The doctors there have never seen or cared for John Paul, whereas Dr. Harmon's knowledge of my son and his condition is indisputable. After much contemplation, we decide to take John Paul back to North Carolina to have the final surgery.

Chapter 18

Our fire-engine-red Suburban is packed, and John Paul is secure in his car seat. It's still early in the morning, and where we're going hasn't been discussed with John Paul yet. For some reason, he thinks we're going to Disney World. His excitement tears at my heart. I wish that's where we were all going. Instead, we're making the eleven-hour drive to North Carolina, where we will stay the night with Annette's parents.

Every few minutes, I glance into the rearview mirror to check on John Paul. His hair is longer than that of most three year olds, but he likes it and so do I. It reminds me of Samson, whose strength was in his long hair. I hope the same may be true for my son.

Watching my son, unaware of what awaits him in North Carolina, I'm filled with a variety of emotions: anxiety, hurt, and helplessness. I begin to wonder if this will be the last week I will be able to see him or touch him. This fear is always present when John Paul goes into surgery. No parent should have to experience this. I wrestle with demons of distress and hopelessness. The only saving grace is my faith. Without it, I'd be lost.

When we turn into his grandparents' driveway, John Paul claps his hands and shouts, "Grandma! Papaw!" He is so happy to see his grandparents that I can't help but watch him. He poses for pictures and smiles. I smile back, but the thought of what tomorrow holds kills the joy of the moment.

The morning of his surgery arrives. Annette and I both find it hard to get out of bed. I walk into the family room. John Paul, an early riser, is already sitting on the floor watching *Barney*. I wish I could freeze time and not have to venture into this new day, but after breakfast we pile into the SUV. John Paul wants to know where we are going and why his grandparents are not coming. I avoid his questions and change the subject.

The drive is short, only about thirty minutes, but it is enough time for us to pray the rosary. John Paul's voice joins in unison with Annette's and mine as he enunciates each word.

I pull into the parking lot and find a space. As I push John Paul's stroller, Annette's hand is tightly clasped around my arm. Reluctantly, we enter the main admitting area, both of us cut up on the inside but trying to outwardly remain strong for our son. I hear my name being called from across the room. I look, and in the distance, I see Sister Dennis. What a blessing. Since the day John Paul was born, she has been by his side in the hospital, visiting, praying, and encouraging us to rely on our faith and God. Her presence relieves some of the apprehension as we sit and wait.

"John Paul George," the nurse calls from the admitting desk.

We follow the nurse to the pediatric floor and enter a room. John Paul looks around and takes everything in, the bed with railings, the teal recliner, and the rolling wooden tray. By this point, he is confused and afraid. I see it in his eyes.

"Look up here," I say, standing below the television mounted on the wall. "You have your very own television."

His demeanor lightens when he sees the television.

"Plus there's a VCR, so you can watch videos." I reach down, pick him up, place him in the middle of the bed, and turn on the television.

Around one o'clock in the afternoon, a nurse enters the room. At the sight of her, John Paul climbs off the bed and jumps onto my lap. She explains that she needs to get an IV started for the catheterization. She asks John Paul to hold out his arm, and he tenses up. He remembers the procedure and starts to squirm. In the process of trying to locate a vein, the nurse pricks his arm. John Paul begins to cry. He shifts closer into my chest, in an attempt to get away from the needle. I have no choice but to hold him down. John Paul realizes I am helping the nurse. He starts to slap me while screaming for me to make her stop. Finally, a vein pops up, and with one last stick, the nurse gets the IV going. His tears subside, but I can see he's frightened. I place John Paul on his bed. Annette sits down beside him and turns the television to one of his favorite shows to help him calm down.

Trying not to display my emotions, I leave the room and enter the men's room around the corner where I weep like a baby. I feel that John Paul has lost faith in me. I am no longer his protector, his trust in me has slipped, and our bond is broken.

Doctors and nurses filter in and out of the room for the rest of the day. Around six o'clock in the evening, Dr. Harmon enters. He is very pleased with John Paul's progress. Most doctors keep a clear-cut doctor/patient relationship, but I can tell our son holds a special place in his heart. He gives Annette and me a form titled "Request for Operation and/or Other Procedures" to read and sign. We have signed these forms in the past, as a signature is required before any procedure can take place. By signing, I give the hospital permission to proceed with the catheterization. I read the risks including bleeding, infection, stroke, and death. Right under that there is a place for the alternatives to this procedure, with the word "none" scribbled on the line. These are such drastic risks, but there is no alternative. With a lump lodged in my throat, I sign the form. Annette signs on the line beside my name as a witness and dates the form.

The next morning at 8:40 AM, a man in pale green scrubs arrives to take John Paul down to the first floor for his catheterization. He stands behind a wheelchair ready to push.

"If it's OK," I say to him, "I'll carry my son."

He gives a nod. I scoop up John Paul, who is already drowsy from the sedative given earlier, into my arms. Annette and I walk him down to the first floor. At the door, the man waits for us to kiss our son and I hand him over with much apprehension. We watch through the small glass window in the door until our son disappears from sight. Neither of us says much on our walk back up to John Paul's room where we wait.

I pace the floor, talk to family, watch television, and do anything to keep my mind occupied. The doctors assured Annette and me that everything would be fine during the procedure; however, when I think about the release form I know there is always that chance….

After several hours, the nurse informs us that John Paul is fine and will be coming to the room within the half hour.

Groggy, the nurses transfer him from the gurney to his bed. We lower our voices and let him rest, but he does not sleep long. He wakes up with a smile on his face and an appetite.

Tomorrow will be a turning point for our family, the last stage of John Paul's Norwood procedure. Although the first stage is very important, the third is the most crucial surgery, seeing if half of a heart can withstand the pressure of doing the work of a whole heart. The blood flow will be routed to the lower part of the body, linking all three stages together.

Dr. Harmon stops by after supper and discusses the findings of the catheterization. He is very pleased and states again that John Paul is a good candidate for the final stage. While he explains what tomorrow will entail, John Paul sits in the middle of his bed and watches television, not comprehending what is being discussed. Once again, a release form is placed in front of me, this time for the open-heart surgery. I scan through the risks: bleeding, infection, and risks of anesthesia, transfusion, stroke, heart attack, death, and kidney failure.

Signing the paper, I cannot fathom what these consequences might mean for my son or what the surgery will hold.

But we will find out.

Chapter 19

Reluctantly, I release John Paul to the surgical nurse. It is finally the day of John Paul's stage-three surgery. This albatross has haunted me for the past three years, day and night. It has hit me at different times, watching John Paul hit golf balls, teaching him to swim, or watching him sleep. I can be having a great day with my son when, suddenly, the reality of what lays ahead pops into my mind. It is hard to shake the reality of such a future. Today the future I have dreaded is here, the final stage of the Norwood procedure, and it scares the life out of me.

Annette and I walk into the surgical waiting room and join our already waiting families. This place is painfully familiar, the place where we waited through the first and second stages of the Norwood surgeries. Everywhere I look, I see people waiting for news. Everyone is dealing with their own worry. In a way, I feel as though I am not alone, but that thought isn't comforting. Although the room is full, there is only the muffled sound of people whispering, flipping through magazines, shifting as they watch a silent television, or the silence of those with eyes closed, who are most likely talking to the man upstairs.

Annette and I know the routine. We sit hand in hand and begin waiting; we will stay this way for the entire day. I wish I were ignorant about the particulars of the surgery—sometimes ignorance is bliss—but I do know and understand. My son's chest will be exposed and a heart lung machine will sustain his life for most of the day. This realization alone is enough to shake my spirit. I think back to three years ago and the angel sent to me in my time of distress. I watch the corridor and look around the waiting room in hopes of his return. I could use a little reassurance.

I try to remain upbeat. I give Annette's hand a tight squeeze and tell her everything is going to be fine. I remind her of all the prayers currently being said for our son. Since his birth, people have united in prayer for John Paul. With just one look at John Paul, I can see the phenomenal power of prayer.

The hours drag. I find myself on edge, continuously watching the hands of the clock move slower than normal. I flip through magazines and books, but nothing helps alleviate the tension. I occasionally walk over to the volunteer who updates families to see if there is any news. Her response is the same each time, "Still in surgery."

By the eighth hour, the waiting game is getting to me. I cannot sit still or eat or drink. I pace constantly around the room trying to keep my mind occupied. Eventually I collapse into a chair, and more time passes.

"There's Dr. Harmon." At the sound of my own words, I leap out of my chair. It has been eleven hours since John Paul entered surgery.

My knees are wobbly, my eyes search the doctor's face for an indication of how things went, and all I see is strain. He stops in front of me and Annette, as our family circles behind us.

"The surgery went well," he says.

The words are music to my ears. It is instant relief. I feel the tears stream down my face. Annette throws herself into me and we stand tightly enfolded. It is difficult to describe how I feel, but the only word that comes to mind is relief, relief that the third and final surgery is behind us. Finally, it is over. Gradually, Annette and I pull apart, turn to the doctor, and listen to the limited details of the surgery. Dr. Harmon explains that John Paul has been through turmoil, his system is in shock, and it will take time for his vitals to stabilize. He is still in the operating room, but once stable, John Paul will be moved to the PICU where we will be able to visit him in an hour. Although we already know it, he reminds us that recovery is crucial. The next twenty to forty-eight hours are critical.

Although I am relieved the surgery is over, it isn't our biggest obstacle. The surgery was major, but it is the aftercare that really determines whether or not the outcome is a success. John Paul is not in the clear yet.

Annette and I go from the surgical waiting room to the PICU waiting area. The room is much smaller, only holding about twenty chairs. It includes a pay phone, and it has a glass window allowing a view into the hallway. A nurse arrives at the door to take us into the PICU, and Annette and I follow.

John Paul's bed is in the middle of the room, directly in front of the nurses' station. I stand back. I wonder if this is the same boy I saw that morning. Unlike the stage two surgery, this time his features have been transformed. His swollen face looks like it will pop at any moment, his eyes are puffy and crusted shut, and he is bruised black and blue. Annette inches closer, kisses him on his forehead, and tells him that she loves him. I am still frozen. This is the worst I have ever seen him look. I can't get past it. I am responsible. I signed the release form.

Annette tugs at me. "Come talk to him. He needs to hear your voice. It will comfort him."

I shake the doubt from my mind and focus on John Paul's healing. For the next fifteen minutes, I sit beside his bed and talk about the things we love to do together. I describe the golf we will play at the club back in Florida and the movies we will see like *George of the Jungle*. I tell him that I cannot wait to take him to the Aero Club, a landing strip near our home, and watch the planes take off and land.

The nurse informs me that the visitation time is up. I hate to leave him. Annette and I both give him a kiss and leave the room. We go back down to the PICU waiting room, where we will stay until we are able to visit again.

It is eleven o'clock. Annette and I are still in the waiting room. The chairs have cushioned seats, but the arms are wooden and hard. I try to get comfortable so I can get a little sleep and do finally doze off. My sleep is restless, with the events of the day playing out in a dream. I hear my name being called but, still groggy, think it's part of the dream and ignore it. I hear my name again, louder this time, and it becomes obvious that this is not a dream. Slowly I open my eyes and try to figure out where I am. In a haze, I see Dr. Harmon.

"John Paul is going back to the OR. He is losing large amounts of blood from the chest tube."

I've woken up from a dream to be thrust into a nightmare. I can hardly think straight. "Are there any other options?" I ask.

He shakes his head, "No, it is imperative that the bleeding be stopped."

Although I know the doctor's response will be noncommittal, I ask anyway, "Is he going to be OK?" All I want is reassurance, someone to say, "Yes, your son is going to be fine."

"There's risk with every surgery, this is no different," the doctor replies. "The risks are greater because of the traumatic surgery John Paul had only hours ago."

I look at Annette and can tell she can't believe this either. Her head rests in her hands. Without looking up, she asks, "Can we see him?"

"He will be going in shortly," says the doctor, "but you may stay with him until we are ready."

Again we wait, this time at John Paul's bedside, until he leaves the PICU. I can hardly bear to watch him leave again to go into surgery. I start to argue silently with myself. What in the world was I thinking? I should have gone with my initial instinct and taken him to Philadelphia or Boston. I was wrong for not going to a larger children's hospital. Aftercare is so important. Did I not learn anything from previous experiences? Is this hospital going to be able to handle my son's condition?

Annette and I go back to the waiting room. Exhaustion settles in and neither of us can keep our eyes open. We nod off only to wake every few minutes. At two o'clock in the morning, Dr. Harmon stops by and informs us that John Paul is on his way back to the PICU. The surgery was successful. The bleeding has stopped.

The news is great, but I am afraid to show any signs of relief for fear of what is around the next corner.

At 2:30 in the morning, I send Annette back to the waiting room to get some rest. The nurse encourages me to do the same. Visiting hours ended long ago. Annette and I have decided, regardless of the official visiting hours schedule, that one of us will be with John Paul at all times. I am sure that the nurse does not like our self-made rules, but with our son's well-being at stake, there are more important things to worry about than what other people think. I pull up one of the rolling stools and sit directly next to John Paul's bed. I watch everything being done to John Paul in silence.

The nurse begins her vitals check by taking John Paul's temperature, blood pressure, and checking for a pulse in each extremity. She stops and pauses. Her hand moves up and down John Paul's left leg.

"Is something wrong?" I ask.

"I can't find a pulse in the left leg." She takes her stethoscope and listens for a pulse. She notes that the leg is very cold, tense, and discolored.

"Why would that happen?" I get up and clasp my hand around the calf muscle, which is cold. I move my hand to his thigh and find the same thing.

"It may be the arterial line," the nurse explains. "That is a very small tube that is placed in a blood vessel. We use it to check blood pressure, draw blood samples, and check oxygen saturations."

"Can it be removed?" I ask.

"It can, but it will need to be placed elsewhere."

Again my thoughts chase each other. *How did this happen? What if the pulse doesn't return?* No circulation means the leg will die. *Dear God, my son may lose his leg.* Disbelief runs through me. Scenarios of my son not being able to walk, run, or play golf begin to flash through my mind. I cannot help thinking this is something that could have been avoided.

I watch intently as the doctor changes the arterial line. After he finishes, I ask the nurse for a blanket. Methodically, I wrap the left leg with the blanket and begin to massage John Paul's leg in an attempt to revive the circulation. I massage his leg so much that my hands become numb. Although the leg begins to warm up, there is still no pulse. The "what ifs" rage through my mind, driving me crazy, so I try to focus all my energy on rubbing and massaging my son's lifeless leg, keeping the "what ifs" from taking over.

The only way I can tell how much time has passed is by the shift change, as a new nurse arrives around 6:30 AM. The two nurses discuss the events since surgery and the entries on John Paul's chart. I listen, reliving those nightmarish events. I hope the light of day brings better news for John Paul.

Lab results arrive just before the nurses finish their charting. I can see concern spread across both of their faces.

"How are the results?" I inquire of them.

The two look at each other. Then one nurse comes over and shows me the results.

"John Paul's liver enzymes are extremely elevated."

"What does that mean?"

"It can be many things. I will notify the doctor, and he will be in shortly."

I take a break from massaging John Paul's leg and sit on the rolling stool, depleted. I hear the automatic doors open and see Annette. I know she's coming with the hope that John Paul is improving, so I force a smile as she gets closer.

She leans in, gives me a gentle kiss on the cheek, walks over, and kisses John Paul on his forehead.

"How is he?"

It is bad enough to have to tell her about John Paul's leg, but now on top of that there is the issue with the liver enzymes.

"Why's his leg wrapped up?" She reaches under the blanket, touches that leg, and then touches his right leg.

"Derek, his left leg is a lot cooler than his right. What's wrong?" I place my arm around her shoulder and pull her away from John Paul's bed.

"Early this morning the nurse noticed that John Paul's left leg was cold, and she couldn't find a pulse. Evidently the line used to get blood samples, check blood pressure, and oxygen levels injured his leg."

Annette's face is ashen. "What does that mean? Is he going to lose his leg?" Tears begin to flow.

I enfold Annette tightly in my arms. "I am not sure. I hope the blanket will keep it warm, I've been massaging it, trying to revive circulation. It is a bit warmer now. We will have to wait and see if a pulse returns."

I hesitate. I do not want to tell her about the blood work, but I cannot keep anything from her. "There's more," I explain.

"I've only been asleep a few hours," she says. "How can there be more?"

I release my embrace and step back until we are facing each other: "John Paul's liver enzymes are too high."

Her brow crinkles as she tries to understand. "Can't they give him some medicine for that?"

"I am not sure. First they have to find out why the levels are elevated. The doctor should be here any minute."

Annette looks over at his fragile, still body and the machines breathing for him.

"How can John Paul endure all this?"

I shake my head. I, too, am at a loss.

In a time of crisis, the last look you want to see on the face of your child's doctor is one of confusion. But that's exactly what we see when Dr. Harmon comes in. My nerves begin to unravel.

"To be honest," he says. "I am not sure why the liver enzymes are elevated. It can be one of many things. I have ordered an ultrasound of the heart to see if there is a connection. I will know more once the scan is complete."

"When will the ultrasound be done?" I ask.

"X-ray will be up within the next thirty minutes." Dr. Harmon examines John Paul, listens to his heart, and pinches his fingernails and toenails measuring the blood flow to the limbs. When he gets to the left leg, there is nothing. The only warmth left is from the blanket, and the blood flow has stopped. Dr. Harmon places his arms around us both. He can see the effect that this news is having on us. "Hang in there," he says, "And pray."

I nod, as the lump in my throat keeps me from being able to speak, but my thoughts still race. I am terrified that the liver is not functioning because the heart is not pumping enough blood to the lower part of the body.

The X-ray doctor enters the PICU. Dr. Harmon gives him instructions and then walks over to the nurses' station. The doctor rolls the heavy machine next to John Paul. Annette cannot handle the pressure and decides to go to the waiting room. I stay so at least one of us will be here.

The machine takes a few minutes to warm up. Finally, the doctor pushes the button for "record" and starts the scan. I watch the monitor as well as his face. My mind wanders back to Annette's first sonogram and the technician's face when she found the defect. I am on pins and needles, and my heart is racing.

"How does the heart look?" I finally ask.

He does not answer right away, continuing with the scan. I am on the edge. I want to shout, "Hey, that's my son, have a little compassion!" I realize, however, that I am overreacting and settle down and allow him time to look. I wait a few minutes.

I clear my throat. "How does the heart look?" I ask again.

He looks a bit longer, and then responds, "The heart looks fine. I do not see any abnormalities, but Dr. Harmon will review the tape."

There is a certain sense of relief knowing that the heart is OK, but I can see puzzled looks being exchanged between the nurses and residents who are watching. The doctor begins to shut down the machine. He cannot leave. The underlying reason for the elevated liver enzymes has not been resolved.

"Can you please scan the liver?"

The doctor, evidently not used to taking directives from family members, ignores me. I make my request again, "Please, before you leave, scan the liver."

He proceeds to inform me that the doctor only ordered a scan of the heart. He will need orders from Dr. Harmon to scan the liver. I look over my shoulder to see that Dr. Harmon is no longer at the nurses' station. I cannot wait for him to be paged, so I plead, "Please, I beg you. I will take full responsibility, just take a look at the liver."

He hears the direness of my tone and agrees to scan the liver. He squirts gel on to John Paul's abdomen and locates the liver with the scanner. Carefully, he watches the monitor. His eyes remain fixed on the screen while his hand moves, locating every angle. Without a word, he places the scanner back into the slot.

"I'll be right back."

My eyes follow him over to the nurses' station. I watch him pick up the phone, speak into it, and then walk back in my direction.

"Dr. Harmon will be right in."

Within minutes, Dr. Harmon is at John Paul's bed. The two converse while they view the findings. I feel the tension.

Dr. Harmon turns to me, "John Paul has a clot in his liver. This is the reason for the elevated enzymes."

"Can't the clot be dissolved with a blood thinner?"

"I'm afraid it is not that easy. If John Paul is given a blood thinner, he could bleed to death due to his recent surgery. With the rapid deterioration of his liver functions, John Paul is at risk of going into shock, plus his kidneys may not be able to withstand the pressure."

I let out a deep sigh, close my eyes, and pray: *Dear God, what are we going to do? It kills me to look at John Paul. Just days ago he was hitting golf balls, enjoying life to the fullest, and now....*

I can't passively sit back and let things happen. I begin to roam the floors of the ICU like a madman, assertively encouraging each doctor to find out what can be done to save my son. Things move too slowly. Slow motion does not work for me, not when my son's life is at stake. I do not remember the last time I had something to eat, yet my energy level is high. I am running on pure adrenaline. I go back and forth to the offices of the doctors and residents. I hammer them continuously, persuading them to call Boston, Philadelphia, Miami, or any major medical facility to find out how to treat the clot in John Paul's liver.

I enter the PICU doctor's office and together we search the internet for answers. Surely, one of these avenues will yield a possible response. Unfortunately, a blood thinner is the only known solution. This occurrence is such a rarity that there doesn't seem to be any alternative. The other hospitals cannot believe this stroke of bad luck, but no one is able to help.

My adrenaline rush subsides. Annette and I sit by John Paul's bedside and wait. No words are spoken as we stare at our son. I am sure the same worrisome thoughts that float through my mind are floating through Annette's. The confines of a hospital allow for a great deal of time to think. I can't help but think back to the past year and a half, during which I have tried to help John Paul become stronger. I learned a great deal about the body while serving in the South African Military when I was a PTI. That knowledge has been beneficial in helping my son. I encouraged John Paul to do exercises, hoping to get his body in shape for the surgery. I never told my family or friends about the motivation for this daily exercise routine, but I knew it was crucial for John Paul's stamina and strength. I hope it has paid off.

Minutes seem like hours. I am continuously in conversation with doctors in hopes they may find a new remedy. My concern now is not only the liver but also how much time is left until the kidneys begin to fail. Time is short. The nurse notifies me that John Paul's urine output has diminished drastically; this is worrisome.

Pediatric renal dialysis is quickly notified, as are Annette and I, as to what is about to happen. My son is going to be put on dialysis. I try not to think about the people I have known who have been put on dialysis, because these outcomes were not positive. To me, this seems like the beginning of the end. So many machines are providing what my son needs to live that I begin to wonder if he'll be able to survive without them.

Chapter 20

The mundane atmosphere of the hospital gnaws at me. Doctors and nurses chart information, take vitals, draw blood, yet the primary problem still has not been addressed. I cannot let time slip by. Each minute counts. I walk over to the desk and ask the nurse to page Dr. Harmon.

My son is a fighter. He has proven himself on more than one occasion. I think about how it has always been a chore getting John Paul to eat. I think back to a Sunday morning when we were at my parents' home and had just finished breakfast. I decide it is time for John Paul to eat his first egg. I place him in his high chair, mash the egg, and do the entire pep talk routine. I watch his face. As soon as I scoop up a spoonful, he begins to shake his head no and holds up his hands to stop me.

"Here comes the airplane," I say. I swirl my hand around, and just as the plane full of egg is about to land it is suddenly diverted to the floor and a loud scream echoes throughout the room. John Paul is not happy. To this day I can still see his beet-red face. Tears flow, but I gather more egg on the spoon.

"No, Dad, no egg!" his voice demands through his whimpers.

"John Paul, eggs are good for you." This time there is no airplane gliding in the sky, because John Paul is too clever. Now the entire family is in the kitchen doing stunts to capture John Paul's attention. Somehow, I manage to get the spoonful of egg in his mouth.

The surprise plastered on his face is priceless; however, his true willpower and fighter instincts reveal themselves. I watch in disbelief as he refuses to swallow the egg. Instead, he leaves his mouth wide open, holds the egg under his tongue, and cries.

"John Paul, swallow the egg," I insist.

He shakes his head no. For the next ten minutes—yes, ten minutes—he holds his mouth open, the egg still in position. He is determined not to eat the egg. Finally, I concede. I cannot stand to see him cry. I take a napkin, clean the egg from his mouth, lift him out of his high chair, and watch as he runs to play. I know my son is a fighter. I hope that will be enough.

"I can't help but think that if I suggest just the smallest amount of blood thinner, maybe that will break up the clot," I say. I look from Dr. Harmon, then back at John Paul, and continue: "But I have a conflicting thought. What if instead of breaking up the clot, the blood thinner releases the clot and causes a heart attack. Either way the odds are not in his favor. My son is caught in a Catch-22."

Dr. Harmon weighs the suggestion but does not speak. He walks back over and looks at the latest labs. "The labs have not improved, the liver enzymes continue to elevate, and urine output with the dialysis has not shown significant improvement. I have to tell you, if John Paul's liver enzymes do not decrease and his urine output does not increase, the consequences will be fatal. I suggest a low dosage of heparin, a blood thinner administered intravenously. At present this is our only option. There is no other viable alternative."

I look at my son. Something has to be done, and I cannot stand around hoping things will work out. It does not happen that way. The odds are stacked against John Paul. Even though he's a fighter, he can't fight this one on his own. I have to help him. With no other alternative, I give permission to start the drug.

Within minutes, the nurse orders and administers the drug. Once again, Annette and I find ourselves waiting. The wait does not get easier as time progresses. I think about life and the amount of time spent waiting, waiting in traffic, at stoplights, in the grocery store, at the bank, and at the doctor's office. Those trivial wait times cannot compare to waiting for life-or-death results for your child.

The first lab results since administering heparin show no change. The liver count has not increased, but it has not decreased either. I tell myself this is a positive result and trust the next labs will start to show improvement.

The next lab result arrives late in the afternoon. The liver enzymes count has decreased and the urine output has increased slightly. The results confirm that the drug is dissolving the clot. I clutch Annette's hand tightly. Finally, John Paul is heading in the right direction. It is hard to believe, but the next few days are smooth sailing. I am on top of the world. My son is on the mend. I begin to see a light at the end of the tunnel. John Paul is slowly taken out of his drug-induced coma and gradually becomes more aware of his surroundings.

Annette arrives from her makeshift sleeping quarters around 6:30 in the morning. She encourages me to go and get some rest. During our conversation, Dr. Harmon and residents arrive on their morning rounds. They examine John Paul, and discussion follows. The news is great! Today John Paul will be extubated (meaning that the ventilator will be removed), allowing him to begin breathing on his own, a huge step in the recovery process. Annette and I are both anxious and thrilled. Time is not wasted; by eight o'clock in the morning the tube is removed. All that remains is a facial oxygen mask. The large protruding tube is gone! By ten o'clock, my little boy is sitting up in his bed and smiling. I am feeling like a million bucks. Annette's mom walks into the PICU, and John Paul gives a big wave, lifts the oxygen mask up, and says, "Hey, Grandma!"

I am in awe, as is everyone in the PICU. It is hard to believe that this is the same little boy who was fighting for his life just days ago. I am relieved, but then comes the realization that I am exhausted. Annette once again encourages me to go get some rest. This time, I take her advice.

Chapter 21

I walk into the room that has become my bedroom, close the blinds, and get comfortable, or as comfortable as someone can get on a vinyl couch. A certain peace overcomes me now that John Paul is doing better. I can finally rest. I fall into a deep sleep.

I am awakened suddenly by the sound of Annette screaming my name. I awake in horror, leap to my feet, and try to remember where I am. I see Annette at the door panicking. I do not even take time to ask her what is wrong. I rush past her to get to the PICU as quickly as I can. *Dear God! What has happened?*

John Paul is no longer sitting up in the bed smiling or waving. No, he is now lying down with a team of doctors and nurses surrounding him. I rush to the bed, but when the nurse sees me she asks that I wait outside. I don't think so.

"What are they doing to him?" I ask.

"John Paul is being reintubated."

"Explain to me why the tube is being reinserted. When I went to lie down, John Paul was doing fine without the ventilator. What happened?"

By this time, Annette is at my side. She points to a person whom I have never seen before and tells me that he tried to change the arterial line in John Paul's neck. Annette tells me that she tried to explain about John Paul's fear of doctors and needles, but the resident got John Paul into a state and, unable to calm him down, tried to continue the procedure anyway.

"I need Dr. Harmon paged immediately," I demanded.

"Dr. Harmon is in surgery. Dr. Mays is covering."

"Then page Dr. Mays immediately!"

I stand and watch respiratory doctors attempt to stabilize my frail son. Annette stands near the door. She has been upset enough, and this episode is pushing her close to the edge. I look at her. For the first time, I notice how much weight she has lost and the hollowness of her eyes. I am not only worried for my son but also for my wife. I do not know what to do. Each time I think I see a glimmer of light at the end of the tunnel it is abruptly zapped out.

I am in a dust storm of doctors and nurses frantically whizzing around, doing everything possible to save John Paul. Dr. Mays enters the room, stunned at the vision before him. He does not ask questions but immediately takes control of the situation. Within fifteen minutes, John Paul is reintubated and back in a drug-induced coma.

My frustrations erupt. This situation could have been avoided. Now my son is at death's door.

Dr. Mays, Annette, and I enter a small conference room. Annette and I sit on the end of the couch across from the doctor. I begin the conversation.

"Negligence is the reason that my son is fighting for his life. He was fine until the resident starting working on him. Annette explained to the resident that John Paul is afraid of doctors and needles and to take it easy and not get John Paul agitated. From this day forward, I do not want any residents near my son."

The doctor understands my concern and affirms that particular resident will not be allowed to care for John Paul. He does say, however, that being a teaching hospital, it will be hard not to have residents work with John Paul. I do not back down. I reinforce my wish that as hard as it may be, no residents or interns are to work on my son.

This situation extended John Paul's hospital stay by a month but, more importantly, it almost cost him his life.

Chapter 22

Suddenly, the hospital administrative personnel are surrounding my family constantly. Our every need is now a top priority. Unfortunately, this newfound interest has not been driven by compassion or kindness but by fear of a lawsuit. The incident with the resident was preventable. The mistake that almost cost my son his life has, unnecessarily, increased his hospital stay. Annette and I contemplate the lawsuit issue but push it aside. We are grateful. God has been good to us, spared our son, and we do not feel that the added pressure of a lawsuit would be beneficial to us or John Paul right now.

At my request, John Paul is moved to a private room in the PICU, and the night brings a fragment of stability. Annette and I have been at the hospital since the surgery. I refuse to go to the Ronald McDonald House directly across the street. I can't leave the building, even if it is just across the street. My place is with my son. Annette and I take shifts. I take the night and she takes the day. The social worker and administrator have given up on their endeavor to steer us to the Ronald McDonald House. Instead they offer a room at the end of the ICU hall, which includes a storage area for chairs with one vinyl couch. It's not much, but it serves the purpose.

I dim the lights on John Paul's bed and sit in the chair next to him. I think about the past three years. I rehash the good times like his first word. Unfortunately his first word wasn't dad but rather Bo, the name of our neighbor's golden retriever. Bo arrived every day at our sliding-glass door to visit John Paul. I think of John Paul's first-birthday party, the first time he saw Mickey Mouse, and his first Christmas. These moments make me smile, but the events of the day chase away any positive feelings. I have been forced to take a more assertive role in my son's care, to make decisions, and to fight for things when it feels like there is no good option. I feel as if I have added twenty years to my life just in this one day. I am not sure how much more I can take. My body is drained physically, mentally, and emotionally. Yet I know that I still have to persevere for the sake of my son.

I am not sure of the time. I know it's late because there's not much movement in the NICU. I use the down time to try to settle my nerves. I pick up the cassette tapes from the table: UB40, James Taylor, Elton John, the Beatles, and the Bee Gees. I insert the Bee Gees tape into the cassette player and place it beside John Paul's bed so that he is able to hear it. The soothing sound relaxes me. I feel a sense of calm. I flip through a magazine, but then the tape stops, so I reach up and turn it over to the other side and hit "play." A respiratory therapist walks toward the door and enters. It is not the regular therapist but someone I have not met before. It has been a long day, and because the suctioning routine usually does not affect John Paul, I do not bother getting up to greet her.

The young woman is dressed in the royal blue respiratory attire, with her dark hair tightly secured in a ponytail. I say hello and inform her that John Paul is on a blood thinner. I am precise in my explanation, not knowing if she has been briefed on my son's condition. I have learned not to assume anything.

She walks over to the sink, loads her palms with soap, washes her hands, and dries them thoroughly. She hums along with the music while meticulously arranging her utensils in preparation for the procedure. I watch her slowly insert the tube down through John Paul's nose with care. Then I lean my head on the back of the chair, close my eyes, and meditate.

All of a sudden, a shriek reverberates throughout the room. My eyes jolt wide open. I am shaken, in total disbelief of the scene I see playing out before me. Everything seems to be in slow motion. I watch as blood travels up the tube and spews out of John Paul's nose. This can't be! I am in a tailspin; my body is in a state of shock. The therapist doesn't know what to do. She continues to push the tube further down, suctioning and agitating the situation. She will not stop.

I leap to my feet. "What are you doing?"

Instead of removing the tube, she frantically continues to suction and jab deeper.

"Take it easy!"

The words barely have time to depart my lips. Suddenly a gush of blood erupts out of the tube. I watch my son's blood splatter toward the wall and floor. The crisp, white bed linens have become blemished with crimson. The therapist's face is pallid and laced with speckles of blood, her hands shuddering uncontrollably, as the blood continues to surge all over the therapist and onto the floor. She grasps the tube tighter, her eyes rapidly searching around the ICU for help. No one is in sight. Her voice bellows in vain for anyone. There is no response. My insides feel like I'm being thrust into the cockpit of a 747 that's spiraling out of control.

"We're losing him!" she cries out.

I don't know what to do. I glare out into the hallway. No doctor or nurse is in sight. I turn back to face more horror. Blood begins to seep out of John Paul's mouth.

Please someone shake me and wake me from this nightmare. I can't take it anymore! I'm watching my son bleed to death.

I feel as if panic is running through every inch of my body. Then out of nowhere a warm sensation filters through me, the same warmth I experienced three years earlier. I feel calmness and a sudden sense of control.

I move to the therapist and place my hand on her arm. Her bloodshot eyes are hollow. She is unsure of what to do.

"Calm down, everything's gonna be all right. Slowly pull the tube out." I listen to the words exit my mouth, yet I am not sure from where these words are coming.

She feels the same calm, and slowly her shaking hands retract the tube. I tighten my hand around her arm and ask her to back off, hoping the bleeding will stop. Side by side we stand, scared senseless, holding our breath. I hear nothing except the loud beat of my heart thumping hard against my chest. Minutes seem like hours, but then it happens, the bleeding subsides. I can't believe my eyes. I exhale relief with the last bit of breath in me. Tears run down the therapist's face and her bottom lip quivers. She attempts to speak but is unable to do so.

The NICU doctor rushes from another patient's bedside into the room. He stops and takes notice of what looks like a war zone. Winded from the ordeal, I can barely talk. The therapist gains her composure and gives details as the doctor begins to attend to John Paul. I walk over to the sink, wet a cloth, and wipe the blood from John Paul's mouth and swollen face. The therapist pulls numerous paper towels from the dispenser, wets them, and then gets down on her hands and knees and begins cleaning the blood from the floor. I stumble away from the bed. My legs buckle. I drop to my knees and help her clean up my son's blood.

After everyone leaves the room, I sit on the edge of John Paul's bed. Something miraculous had happened, just like it happened three years prior in the wee hours of the morning after John Paul's first surgery. Another miracle. How else can it be explained? There is no other explanation for how the bleeding stopped. I notice the blood stains on my clothes. Even though I have washed my hands there are still remnants of blood under my nails.

I look at John Paul, oblivious to the chaos. My eyes scan the ventilator tube protruding from his small mouth. His body remains still as a statue from the drug-induced coma. I cannot believe this little boy's fate, an obstacle at every turn. Not even a few hours can pass without a jolt of uncertainty striking. I am shattered, not for myself but for my son. The third stage, the final stage of the Norwood procedure, posed more complications than we ever could have imagined.

I have to wonder, will he remember all he has endured, the trauma? Will it affect his life, his dreams?

Chapter 23

John Paul is finally extubated. After weeks of being in the PICU, he is moved to the pediatric floor. The drugs have been tapered off, and he is awake after being in the drug-induced coma for three weeks. His body and muscles are weak. He resembles a Raggedy Ann doll. I prop pillows around him so that he can sit up, but he is not the same little boy who came to the hospital with us. He sits in a daze most of the day, his face blank. I turn the television to his favorite show, but even then he just stares blankly into space. I start to wonder if maybe there has been brain damage, but I push this thought aside, keeping it to myself.

I tell jokes, dance, and sing anything to boost John Paul's morale. The response is the same. I search my brain thinking of things to lift his spirit. He loves the outdoors, so I speak to the doctor and make arrangements to take him outside once or twice a day. Annette and I prop him up in his stroller and walk around outside. We walk around the gardens, up and down the sidewalks. Sometimes we sit under shade trees and let him soak up the fresh air, but most of the time he sleeps. I hope being outside, feeling the heat of the sunlight, the flutter of the breeze, the chirp of the birds, and the noises of everyday life will help him heal.

Nighttime is the worst. Panicky screams pierce the darkness. Annette and I jump out of the hospital chairs that have become our makeshift bed. I turn on the light above John Paul's bed. His screams intensify, his legs kick, and his arms wave erratically in front of him. This is not the first night that this has happened. It has become a routine occurrence. Every night around one or two o'clock in the morning it starts. It is terrifying because he cries nonstop. I do not know what is causing him to do this. Even the nurses cannot offer an explanation.

Is it nightmares? Nightmares about all he has endured? There is no way to know, and all I can do is try to pacify him. Annette and I both try holding him, comforting him, singing to him, but nothing works. Finally we put him in his stroller and roam the halls of the pediatric ward for two or three hours, and for some reason this calms him. As soon as the stroller stops he begins to scream. I try to figure out why the stroller ride is calming. When John Paul was a baby Annette would push him in his stroller until he fell asleep. Maybe he reverts back to his infancy, and the movement of the stroller comforts him. It is only later as I read the nursing notes that we find out the cause of the hysteria.

Chapter 24

Withdrawal, side effects of the drugs, or a central nervous system impairment caused by an air pocket in a vein are all listed in John Paul's notes as the possible causes of his nightmares. None of these are ever discussed with us. When we ask the cause of these nighttime episodes the staff seems baffled. No one ever explains these issues or the side effects of the high-powered narcotics administered to John Paul, but we are going to find out.

For the last two months, he has been receiving nutrition intravenously. Some of the simple tasks he's already mastered have to be reintroduced, such as learning to sip. Annette and I were criticized greatly by friends for giving John Paul the soft drinks Coke and Sprite at the ages of two and three, but we had our reasons. These two soft drinks, loaded with calories, helped put weight on John Paul and built him up for the third surgery.

I know how much John Paul loves Sprite. I take a straw and squirt a little in his mouth. His taste buds ignite, and I watch with delight as he smacks his lips together and motions for more. Slowly he is reunited with some of his favorite foods. I feel better as he begins to eat, because I know that with each bite he will begin to get his strength back.

Dr. Harmon stops by to visit and check on John Paul. He begins the conversation by asking about John Paul's intake. This is important. In fact, at every doctor visit the first question has always been an inquiry into John Paul's intake. If he is eating, his body can thrive and heal. I happily report that John Paul has been eating better with each passing day. The doctor is pleased, but then says something that blindsides both Annette and I.

"From this point forward, John Paul cannot have salt," the doctor says.

I ask if he said low salt or no salt. He clarifies that he said no salt. He will have a dietician come by and speak to Annette and me about a healthy diet for John Paul. Wow. I think about a diet with no salt. Almost absolutely everything has salt: bread, milk, cheese, not to mention the things most kids love like chips, chicken nuggets, and McDonald's hamburgers. I have to wonder, what is my son going to eat?

The discharge day is in sight, with only one more hurdle to clear, the issue of how to administer a blood thinner at home. While in the hospital the heparin given to break up the clot in the liver and prevent future clots has been administered intravenously. We now face the challenge of finding a drug that can be given to John Paul at home. Most blood thinners are geared toward an older patient. The doctor tells us the only option is to give John Paul a high-powered blood thinner called Coumadin. Dr. Harmon explains that we will have to monitor the thickness of John Paul's blood daily. I can't imagine how I am going to monitor the thickness of his blood daily. It's hard to fathom taking him each day for blood work. I know how scared he is of needles. The thought of him having to be stuck daily makes me sick to my stomach.

"You will monitor his blood at home," the doctor says.

I picture what his words mean. I, not a nurse, will have to collect blood samples daily. I have seen how John Paul panics and works himself into a state when a nurse attempts to draw blood. Now I will be the one who sticks John Paul. I am shell-shocked. I thought that inserting a feeding tube when he was a baby was bad. This is different. John Paul is older and aware of what is going on. I cannot comprehend what this will do to him. He will hate me, never forgive me, and lose all faith in me.

Catching up with the conversation, I hear the doctor say a coagulation monitor will need to be purchased. The monitor determines the clotting time of John Paul's blood, which is extremely important. Coumadin, the drug being prescribed, is an adult drug and not intended for children. Therefore John Paul will have to be watched closely to make sure that his blood does not get too thin. If that happens something as simple as a sneeze can cause internal bleeding. The bleeding is deadly because it can go undetected and not be discovered until it is too late.

"There has to be something else we can give John Paul. This drug seems too strong," I say, thinking out loud.

Dr. Harmon reiterates that Coumadin is the only solution and that everything should be fine as long as we monitor the results closely. He leaves an information brochure on the monitor and states that he will have one available tomorrow.

Knowing the task that awaits me when John Paul comes home diminishes my joy at his discharge, but I will do anything for my son, and if this is what it takes to get him out of the hospital and home, then so be it. We will work through this just as we have worked through everything else.

Chapter 25

John Paul is out of the hospital. All three stages of the Norwood procedure are now complete. I have felt many different things throughout this process, but the one I feel now is by far the best. At last I can breathe. A weight has been lifted from my shoulders.

We will be in North Carolina for two weeks. Then John Paul goes back for his postoperative checkup. The mood at Annette's parents' house is jubilant. John Paul is home! I hope that being in a familiar environment will encourage healing so that I will begin to see hints of the "before surgery" John Paul.

Unfortunately, the night terrors continue, as does the nonresponsiveness. He is not completely unresponsive, even beginning to talk more with each passing day, but something is still not right. Annette and I sit on the front porch swing. John Paul sits on Annette's lap. My niece, Leigh-Ann, whom John Paul calls La, walks on to the porch. I put my finger to my lips and motion for her to keep quiet.

"John Paul, who just walked outside?"

He does not answer right away, but finally he says, "Grandma."

Annette and I look at each other. I stand up in front of him and Annette asks, "John Paul, who is standing in front of you?"

"Kia," he responds. Kia is his nickname for his Aunt Cecilia.

The air leaves my lungs. I can't breathe. Annette shakes her head and mouths, "*He can't see!*" I think about all that he has been through in the last two months: open-heart surgery, a second surgery for bleeding, a clot in his liver, kidney failure, loss of circulation in his leg, near death, and now blindness. I shake my head in disbelief and try not to let my emotions get the best of me.

I go inside and call our doctor friend John, with whom we've discussed John Paul before. He has a way of calming my nerves, and today is no different. I describe John Paul's symptoms. He tells me that several years ago his wife was on painkillers for multiple sclerosis for an extended period of time. When she stopped the drugs she could not see. This blindness was temporary; within two weeks she regained her sight. This makes me feel better. I know that John Paul has been on high-powered painkillers and more than likely his blindness is a side effect from the drugs, but only time will tell.

A few days pass. It is five o'clock in the morning. Annette and John Paul are up in the family room. I hear muffled sounds from the television. Slowly I get out of bed and walk into the room. John Paul is sitting on Annette's lap. A balloon is floating beside the television. I pull on the ribbon attached to the balloon and out of nowhere John Paul says, "Tigger!"

I look at the television. *Barney*, not *Winnie the Pooh*, is on. I glance at Annette. Her mouth is open in awe.

"Derek, look at the balloon, it is Tigger, the tiger from *Winnie the Pooh*!"

"John Paul, who is holding the balloon?" Annette asks.

"Daddy!"

Annette and I squeeze John Paul tightly. We run up and down the hall waking the entire family and share the good news.

John Paul begins to transform back into the little boy he was before the surgery. He passes his two-week checkup with flying colors. The only drawback is that I have to start checking John Paul's blood next week. The drive back to Florida is a complete 180 from the drive up to North Carolina. I was frightened that my son would not be with me on my return trip, but now I look in the rearview mirror at my son sitting in the back seat. His brown eyes sparkle as our eyes meet. I thank God he is still with me.

The weeks that follow start off positively. The only drawback remains testing John Paul's blood. The repetitiveness does not lessen his anxiety, as his reaction is the same every time he sees the needle—sheer terror. Today, the result shows his blood is too thin. I call the pediatric cardiologist in North Carolina and ask if I should reduce the dosage of Coumadin. The answer is no, stick to the same dosage because sometimes the readings fluctuate. I follow the instructions.

Chapter 26

John Paul is sitting in his stroller and playing with his cousin Leigh-Ann. Suddenly he becomes irritated for no reason, he shouts, and his face turns blood red. I am flabbergasted. I have never seen him like this. He tells me that he is tired and wants to lie down. I take him out of his stroller and place him on the bed where he falls asleep quickly. I tell myself that his erratic behavior was just caused by exhaustion.

I check on him throughout the afternoon. Three hours later, he wakes up but only momentarily. Before long he has fallen back to sleep. At 5:30 PM I wake John Paul and attempt to feed him, but he is so drowsy he cannot even chew the food. I take him back upstairs and lay him on the bed. Within minutes he is back asleep. Annette and I stay in the room and watch him sleep, both of us anxious. At eight o'clock, John Paul is still sleeping. I try to wake him, but it takes me several times to finally rouse him. This is not normal, so Annette and I decide to take John Paul to the emergency room.

The three of us enter the emergency room. John Paul is limp in my arms. The cardiologist on call enters the small room where we wait. I inform her that John Paul has hypoplastic left heart syndrome and has just recently gone through the third stage of surgery. I ask what could be the cause of the sleepiness. The doctor begins to examine John Paul, panicking when his saturations appear on the monitor. I advise her that the cardiologist in North Carolina told me to always look at John Paul, not the number, and his coloring looks great. The low saturations bother her, but she finally focuses on the reason John Paul is in the emergency room.

The official diagnosis is a virus. The treatment: take him home, let him rest, and he should be better in a day or two. Annette and I follow her directives and take our son back home. John Paul sleeps through the night and most of the next day. He wakes up in the late afternoon just long enough to eat a small amount of food before going back to sleep. The next morning I wake around six o'clock to find that John Paul has not moved the entire night. I notice his body twitching and jerking abnormally. I am unable to wake him. I call my friend John. His advice is to get John Paul to the emergency room as soon as possible.

I ride in the ambulance with John Paul, and Annette follows in the car behind us. As soon as we get there, John Paul is rushed into the emergency room. Annette and I are greeted by a young doctor who asks questions about John Paul's symptoms. I explain that John Paul was at this hospital the night before and give a detailed account of what has been occurring. Annette and I stand by John Paul's bed. I watch Annette stroke his hair and whisper in his ear that she loves him. The room is similar to the NICU at the hospital in North Carolina. I can't believe that John Paul is back in this setting. When I left North Carolina I thought the hospital would be a memory of the past, but now this.

The doctor spends a moment getting a sense of John Paul's chart and assures me that my son is in good hands.

Suddenly, John Paul begins to have another seizure-like episode. The doctor observes the ordeal, which only lasts a minute or so. I inform the doctor that the seizures started this morning and have become more frequent.

The doctor does not hesitate. John Paul is immediately rushed to X-ray. Annette and I pace the emergency room corridor, wondering what could be wrong.

The doctor, helping out from a top hospital in Miami, accompanies John Paul back to his room from the X-ray lab. She motions Annette and me to the corner of the room. Her smile from earlier has gone.

"The reason John Paul has been sleeping so much and starting to have seizures is due to a brain hemorrhage." She pauses, giving us time to absorb her words.

All of a sudden, I feel out of my comfort zone. I am not in North Carolina where the doctors and nurses know John Paul, I am twelve hours away. What in the world am I going to do? I do not know anything about this hospital.

She continues: "The hemorrhage is severe. I am afraid there is not much time."

"What do you mean not much time?"

"It is imperative that we get him to surgery immediately in order to release the pressure from the brain. Otherwise John Paul will die."

I will not tolerate the word *die*. That word does not exist in my vocabulary.

"Can we chopper him to Miami?"

"There is not enough time. I have placed a call to the best neurosurgeon on staff. He is not on call, but the staff is trying to locate him." She receives a page and excuses herself.

Annette is emotionally distraught. She is frightened that this facility will not be able to handle John Paul and the severity of his condition. She goes to a phone, dials a number, and pleads to speak to Dr. Harmon. When she tells Dr. Harmon the news, tears stream down her face and her hand holding the phone shakes. After a few minutes she hangs up.

"What did he say?" I ask her.

"Dr. Harmon told me that since we live in Florida we must establish our lifeline here. We must trust the doctors and their ability. He also told me that he will keep the lines open so the doctor can call him with any questions."

My family arrives at the hospital. They have called relatives and friends to start the prayer chain. I watch Annette call her parents in North Carolina. She tearfully tells me that they are on their way down.

I feel a slight touch on my shoulder. I turn to face the doctor.

"The neurosurgeon has been contacted," the doctor says. "He should be here any minute. We are getting John Paul ready for surgery."

Annette and I go to our child's bedside. Once again, our son is in need of a miracle and the odds are not in his favor. Annette does not stop kissing him and whispering words in his ear. She is no longer crying. She is strong and determined to transmit that strength to our son. I stand, watch, and silently pray for another miracle.

The emergency-room doctor informs us that it is time to go. Annette and I accompany John Paul to the operating room. I cannot take my eyes off of him. I absorb his features, long dark eyelashes, full pink lips, smooth skin, and long dark hair. In the recesses of my mind I hear his sweet, innocent voice, his laughter, and I yearn to hear those sounds again. The walk is lengthy, and while on the way, John Paul is gripped by another seizure. Our steps hasten. At the entrance to the operating room, the doctor and nurses pause briefly, allowing us to kiss our son. I watch, as I have many times before, my son disappear into the unknown.

The waiting room consists of ten plastic chairs and a view of a garden and statues. An elderly lady dressed in pink sits at a wooden desk. She is the volunteer who updates families on the status of surgeries. Annette and I pace up and down in front of the windows, stopping every few minutes to look outside. I am shocked when the volunteer states that the surgery is over and the doctor will be out soon. I fear the worst.

I see a tall man in blue scrubs walking down the hallway. A million butterflies flutter in my stomach. Annette grabs my arm tightly, and we both stand as the doctor approaches. Before he introduces himself he relieves our fears.

"John Paul is fine."

Annette and I tearfully break down. It is another prayer answered, another miracle delivered.

The doctor introduces himself and begins to tell Annette and me about the surgery. The difference between life and death for John Paul had come down to just a few minutes. The doctor's face grows pale as he explains that as soon as he drilled a hole in John Paul's skull, the pressure from within released and blood spattered on the wall. Even a slight hesitation would have cost John Paul his life. I still get chills today when I think of what could have been.

The cause of the hemorrhage: John Paul's blood had become too thin from the Coumadin. I told the doctors up north the reading from his blood test, but they told me to keep the same dosage, which could have cost John Paul his life. Something as simple as a sneeze could have triggered the bleeding. This life-threatening event could have been avoided. A simple baby aspirin should have been prescribed instead of the high-powered adult drug.

John Paul's hospital stay lasts several weeks. During that time a new lifeline is established with his new pediatric cardiologist, Dr. Bowen, and the nurses of the community.

The brain surgery robs John Paul of one of his famous attributes, his long locks. After the surgery, we make John Paul wear a bright-yellow bumblebee helmet because we're not taking any chances. The helmet will become his trademark style until his hair grows back.

Physically, emotionally, and mentally, the summer has been a series of catastrophic hurricanes. My only hope is that this will be it, that we've finally made it through this turbulent season.

Chapter 27

Readjusting to Life

When John Paul was young, it was easy to keep him safe and away from sickness, but now he is old enough to start kindergarten. Annette and I face the difficult decision of sending John Paul to school and risking a serious illness or keeping him home, where he might miss out on those life-defining experiences. Both Annette and I enjoyed school. We remember the lifelong friendships and those moments that helped us grow up and learn about life. How could we deny him those experiences? But how could we risk another, possibly life-threatening, hospital stay?

Most people don't seem to understand our hesitation. The surgery is completed, and John Paul is currently healthy. Entering school is just part of the natural process of children growing up. Although that's true, Annette and I know John Paul's life has never followed the "normal" growing-up process. We can still see—vividly—those images of John Paul hooked up to all the machines: the ventilator breathing for him, dialysis machines assisting his kidneys, the induced coma under which he was placed. How could we risk anything medically that even had a chance of sending him back there?

At this point, we've heard all the arguments about how he needs interaction with children his own age and to be in a school setting outside the home. Deep down we know all this is true, but we're not sure it outweighs the medical health concerns. Illnesses other children could take in stride and get over on their own, John Paul wouldn't be able to fight off. As parents of a child with a life-threatening illness, Annette and I are forced to see the world and everyday occurrences in a different light. It may seem like we overthink the simple things, but in reality that's what we have to do. It's one of the ways John Paul has transformed our lives, and we'll do whatever we can to keep him healthy and prospering.

As with every major decision, we search out thoughts and pray about what to do. Then we research our options. We finally find a private kindergarten with only seven students. Even though we're still hesitant, we believe that John Paul will be safer in a small classroom with fewer students.

Once the decision is official, we get to start doing all those typical back-to-school errands together. We take John Paul shopping for new school supplies and clothes. We get to experience his excitement as we count down for the "big day" on the calendar. So far everything is going the way it should.

John Paul has no trouble adjusting to life as a kindergartner. He loves interacting with the other children, and his teacher is a gem. Even at this young age, John Paul has found ways to stand out from the crowd. Once, he made a card for Annette proudly stating his mom was twenty-nine years old. That card made Annette the envy of every mother in the class!

As John Paul flourished in the classroom, however, his health began to suffer. Barely a month into the school year, John Paul contracts bronchitis.

Chapter 28

Our worst fears about sending John Paul to school have become our new reality. He is out of the classroom for weeks, but his health just continues to deteriorate. The pediatrician places him on steroids, antibiotics, and breathing treatments.

Then one evening, I am helping John Paul change into his pajamas when I notice his stomach is distended. I call the pediatrician and cardiologist. Both tell me it is probably a reaction to the steroids or antibiotics. We wait a few days, but his stomach has not changed. If anything, it's bigger. Annette and I are concerned enough that we decide to take him to the emergency room. I hate hospitals. The smell and coldness make me think of the past. Too many bad memories resurface as we arrive. John Paul's fears are greater than mine. I downplay the visit and promise no needles.

John Paul, Annette, and I wait in a small room. Doctors and nurses come and go. Tests and X-rays all come back negative. Even after all the tests, it still seems the cause must be an adverse reaction to antibiotics or steroids. I am told to keep an eye on his condition, and if additional swelling or swelling around the ankles appears I am to bring him in or notify his doctor. We leave the hospital relieved that it doesn't seem to be anything major.

Even though we are continuously told it's nothing major and to just watch for additional swelling, we are concerned when months pass with no change in John Paul's condition. We're planning a trip to North Carolina anyway to cheer on a friend playing in a PGA (golf) tournament, so Annette and I decide this would be the perfect opportunity to get a second opinion on John Paul's condition.

Dr. Reid Keever, Annette's obstetrician, and our family have become close friends. We all meet in Greensboro for dinner. I tell him about John

Paul's distended stomach. He calls my son over and gives him a hug, casually examining his abdomen and then sends him off to play with his children.

"That's not normal," he says.

I tell him the doctor's diagnosis. He explains that John Paul has been off of the medication long enough for it to be out of his system. Something else has to be the cause of his swollen stomach. The worried look on his face makes me sick.

"Is it serious?" Annette asks.

"That I do not know. Why don't you bring him to my office in the morning, and I will do an ultrasound of his abdomen."

Annette and I agree to meet at his office at 9:30 AM in the morning.

The drive from Greensboro back to Annette's parent's home is quiet. John Paul is asleep in the back seat. The last few years have been wonderfully complication free, but now this.

John Paul questions why we are going to Uncle Reid's office. I tell him Uncle Reid wants to take a picture of his stomach and that it will not hurt. He is unfazed by this and happily climbs on the exam table. John Paul is as cool as a cucumber, unlike me. The scan goes on for twenty minutes and covers every inch of John Paul's abdomen.

When the exam is finished, Annette takes John Paul out to the car while I stay and talk to Reid. Just like all the other tests we've had done, these look fine, but something has to be causing the swelling. Reid asks if he can talk to John Paul's cardiologist in Florida. I give him the number.

***

We're still in North Carolina when we hear back from John Paul's cardiologist. He has to have blood work done immediately. Annette takes John Paul to the diagnostics office as quickly as she can. I meet them there with my brother, Gerard.

The screams I hear on entering the office rip at my heart. John Paul's face is crimson red. His fists are clenched, and he's swinging them uncontrollably like a boxer who's dazed and confused. The nurse stands in front of him, needle in hand.

"I won't hurt you, I promise," she says hoping to allay his fear. The words only make him scream louder. He has heard those words before and knows they are lies.

"He doesn't believe you. He knows it will hurt," I say, walking over to John Paul. I kneel in front of him as he sobs breathlessly. I look at Annette and ask, "What happened?"

"The nurse has had to stick him several times. She is unable to find a vein." She pauses. "Should we leave? I can't put him through this."

I shake my head. "We do not have a choice, it has to be done." I glance up at the nurse. "One more try."

The nurse nods and prepares herself.

I grab my son's small arms. "John Paul, you need to calm down." His fear-filled eyes lock with mine. "We have to do this. I need you to be a strong boy."

The nurse takes one step in his direction, and he goes ballistic. Annette, Gerard, and I together restrain him as the nurse inserts the needle into his arm. His legs kick and his body jerks, but within a few seconds the nurse shouts, "I got it!" With the blood finally drawn, all that's left to do is wait for the results.

It is early afternoon when Reid gets the results of the blood work back. John Paul's protein levels are extremely low. Protein is vitally important because it builds, maintains, and replaces tissues and organs. Muscles and the immune system are all made up of mostly protein. After discussing the results with Dr. Bowen, John Paul's doctor in Florida, it's decided that John Paul needs to go in for an appointment as soon as possible.

Annette and I pack up immediately to head back to Florida, scheduling an appointment for John Paul that next morning. During the entire drive there, we rationalize back and forth. If he's losing protein, we just have to feed him more. We'll start him on a diet filled with foods rich in protein like hamburgers, cheese, and milk.

Chapter 29

John Paul sits on the examining table, legs dangling, as he waits for Dr. Bowen. This is one doctor he doesn't mind coming to see, because he knows that Dr. Bowen does not allow needles in his office. He is still too young to comprehend all that is going on. When Dr. Bowen enters the room, his normally wide smile seems diminished and his usual positive, upbeat demeanor is guarded.

The diagnosis is protein-losing enteropathy (PLE), a condition in which protein is lost through the bowels or kidneys. The next step is to verify the source of the loss. Is protein being lost through the bowels or kidneys? I question if the medications, steroids, and antibiotics could be a factor. Dr. Bowen says this is unlikely. Annette and I are even more stunned by what Dr. Bowen tells us is the cause.

PLE is a side effect of the Norwood procedure. In all the years John Paul has been living with his condition, no one has informed us of this possible side effect. After the visit, Annette phones Dr. Harmon to tell him about the complications.

His response, "You have to be very careful placing children who have had the Norwood procedure on antibiotics."

Annette and I mull over this new information. That being the case, why were we not told about this before? Augmentin, the high-powered antibiotic given to John Paul, could have triggered the PLE. This entire complication may have been avoided if Annette and I had been warned about the hazards of antibiotics.

It is discovered that John Paul is losing protein through his bowels. Although the news is not good, it is the lesser of the two evils. Losing protein through his kidneys would have been the more devastating of those options.

Now that we know what's wrong, I begin my mission to find ways to replenish John Paul's body with protein. The first thing I do is ask the doctor if he can take a protein supplement. With his permission, I start John Paul on two protein shakes a day, making sure the rest of his diet is high in protein. It is a challenge. The shakes are bitter, but my son is a trouper, and Annette and I invent ways to spice the shakes up.

The protein settles in his stomach, which means it is not filtering through his body. His stomach continues to get larger, and now the change is noticeable as it begins to bother John Paul. Every time I look at him, I am reminded of the ads on television of the malnourished children in Africa. Their fragile, thin frames are overshadowed by their swollen stomachs. People stare at him, and some even have the nerve to comment on his large stomach. The comments trigger insecurity in John Paul, something that will be as hard for him to overcome as the medical challenges.

***

Things continue this way for four years. I am relentless about trying to find a therapy that will help my son. I call every major medical facility I can think of asking about new drugs or treatments. It's starting to look hopeless, but God works in mysterious ways.

I am in Las Vegas doing a clothing show when one of my fellow reps introduces a new water, Enon. He says the water might even help John Paul because it helps hydrate the cells. I'm not sure, but at this point I am willing to try anything. I call Dr. Bowen and fax him the information on the water. He states that the water will not harm John Paul and to give it a try.

I start John Paul on the water, and through reading the brochure, I find the name of a doctor from Johns Hopkins who helped develop the water. I call and speak to his secretary, explaining John Paul's situation. She immediately puts the doctor on the line.

"Forget the water, I have a drug that will help your son," says the doctor.

His words spark hope. I give him Dr. Bowen's number. Within the hour, Dr. Bowen calls in a prescription for the potassium-sparing diuretic spironolactone. Within a week, the fluid slowly begins to dissipate from

John Paul's stomach. The difference is astonishing! Four years of sticking with this medication have proven beneficial.

God works in mysterious ways, as I said. What a coincidence that a bottle of water placed me on the path to finding the drug that would help John Paul. While spironolactone helps control fluid retention for John Paul, his body continues to have problems absorbing protein. That problem is counteracted by the high-protein diet he started four years ago, but PLE has slowed his growth and he will remain very small.

Although John Paul is now twenty, most people mistake him for someone much younger. As a teenager, people would still offer him a balloon at the grocery store or a sucker at the bank. These misconceptions continue to bruise John Paul's confidence and self-image. It is a tough road for John Paul, not only from a medical perspective but also because of the new obstacles of peer pressure. He wants to be seen as fitting in with the rest of his peers.

My protective instinct doesn't diminish as John Paul gets older. As each year passes, though, I realize that I must continue to loosen my hold and let John Paul grow into the man God has planned for him to be. I must do this even if that means he has to confront and struggle with things from which I'd rather keep him sheltered.

PART II

Homeschooling and Traveling

"If you live to be a hundred, I want to live to be a hundred minus one day so I never have to live without you."

– A.A. Milne, *Winnie the Pooh*

Chapter 1

Kindergarten is the last time John Paul is in a formal school environment. After the bronchitis and all its side effects, we come to the difficult conclusion that the risks outweigh the benefits for our son's life. While trying to determine the best alternative to the classroom, we find that the State of Florida offers a program titled "Hospital/Homebound" for students who have a medically diagnosed condition that is acute or catastrophic in nature and confines them to their home or a hospital for an extended time. This program sounds like an amazing opportunity for John Paul, and we are very excited to be a part of it.

The program will provide John Paul with all the advantages of the classroom—a teacher and a full curriculum—in a controlled environment that won't pose a health risk. We sign John Paul up, and a certified teacher starts coming to our home for five hours every week.

The program seems to be working great. John Paul is staying healthy, loves his teacher, and is getting an education. It isn't until the end of third grade that we start to see problems. John Paul is required to complete the same workload and standardized tests as students receiving thirty or more hours of teacher-led instruction. He is struggling to keep up. The more it looks like he's falling behind, based on the standardized test results, the more stressed Annette and I see him become. Even working as hard as he can, it's not possible for him to meet the same goals.

We know that at the end of the year, the Florida Comprehensive Assessment Test is coming up, and the pressure starts to take a toll on John Paul's health. Even though John Paul has studied extensively, it proves too much for him. This undue stress is not something John Paul needs while trying to stay healthy. Annette and I decide that it's time to look for other options.

Annette starts by contacting the man in charge of the program in our area. He explains that he is sorry for our situation, but he is not able to do anything to improve it. He says, "John Paul just happened to slip through the cracks."

Slip through the cracks? After all the obstacles John Paul has cleared just to survive, that comment makes me feel as if my son is just an afterthought. His disability doesn't make him any less deserving of a good education than healthy kids his age, and he has always wanted to learn. We don't want to see our son penalized for a medical condition over which he has no control. It was a difficult decision for Annette and me to pull him out of school to protect his health. Now it seems that decision means he doesn't get access to the same resources and education as his peers. No child, sick, disabled, or healthy, should "slip through the cracks." The only advice we receive about improving the quality of John Paul's education is to contact our elected officials.

Annette is a fighter and refuses to give up until the system works fairly for John Paul and any other student in similar circumstances. She contacts our congressman, senator, governor, even the president, but all inquiries and concerns fall on deaf ears.

We continued our campaign for a year, but with no responses or improvements in sight we know that we have to change our tactics in the fight for John Paul's education. This is just another hurdle for our family to overcome. The system might have allowed John Paul to fall through the cracks, but we will not allow this to happen. The only other option is homeschooling.

Annette finds a Catholic curriculum for us to follow, and we return to school alongside John Paul. It has been years since I graduated from college, and it isn't an easy task for either of us to recall all the information we learned during our school days. Annette and I divide the subjects based on our individual strengths. My main focus will be math. John Paul is on board with that, as he has already heard plenty of stories about his mom's struggles with math in college. In fact, Annette was actually my first math student when I tutored her in statistics in college. It turned out that was great experience to have had when it came time to teach John Paul. He often joked that if Mom could pass math, so could he!

Chapter 2

Although John Paul enjoys math, history is his favorite subject. He has always loved watching movies, reading, and learning about events that took place in different time periods. At an early age, he began sporting a coonskin Davy Crockett hat. He would sit for hours in front of the television and watch the sagas of the "king of the wild frontier" while singing the theme song at the top of his lungs.

To nurture John Paul's love of history, we try to take trips to historic sites. The Crockett TV show and music bring back memories of our trips to Texas, where John Paul actually got to visit the Alamo.

While John Paul is in school, my job as a clothing representative for my store's southwest and southeast territory includes a great deal of travel. Not wanting to leave Annette and John Paul alone so often, and with John Paul now out of a traditional school schedule, it only makes sense to travel as a family. We use these trips as a way to supplement his education, giving him "classroom" experiences outside of the house.

One of the concerns we had about homeschooling John Paul is that we will be missing out on the diversity of the classroom. Homeschooling makes it much harder for him to meet and interact with people from different cultures or backgrounds, but with the opportunity to travel together we are able to give John Paul those experiences in a different way. Through these trips, John Paul is introduced to people of all ages and from every walk of life. He not only learns about but also gets to experience the different cultures of the places he visits. Through that exposure, he learns important diversity lessons: Every person has value, never judge based on race or appearance, and always treat every person with respect and dignity. The added benefit is that all of this can happen in a somewhat controlled environment where Annette and I can keep him healthy.

We would have loved for John Paul to be able to attend school, learn in a classroom, meet friends and do things with them, and experience a more "normal" life. There will always be some regret that John Paul was unable to do this. In some ways, John Paul's life is still limited no matter how many opportunities we try to give him. As a parent, my heart aches for him in that respect. Although John Paul lives the life he has to the fullest, Annette and I sometimes wonder if he has really been able to experience life to the fullest.

Chapter 3

John Paul sometimes interacts differently with society than other kids his age, but I don't believe he has been hindered in any way. The empathy of so many people has encouraged him to be more empathic to others and their needs. His socialization has been unconventional, but it has been effective. John Paul has had the opportunity to meet and work with some very unique people. Like any other parent of a child with a disability, Annette has experienced the heartache of knowing there are things that John Paul won't be able to do. So, she tries to create unique, once-in-a-lifetime experiences to compensate for the ordinary ones he cannot have.

***

From Annette

One of these experiences was to go see Tyler Perry's play *Madea's Big Happy Family,* in Jacksonville, Florida. As we make it to our seats, only a few rows back from the stage, I get a call on my cell phone. Mr. Perry's assistant asks that she and John Paul meet at the stage. John Paul is ecstatic. We arrive at the stage, and in just a few seconds, Tyler Perry's assistant takes us behind the curtain.

"Mr. Perry will be arriving shortly," she says. "Once he arrives, he will meet with you for a few minutes in his dressing room. Before he gets in costume he has prayer with the cast members. He would like for you guys to join him for the prayer as well. Is that OK?"

"We would be honored," I say, as I look at John Paul and smile.

Once inside Tyler Perry's dressing room, the first thing John Paul notices is the Madea costume. The sight of that puts him in Madea mode.

Mr. Perry offers him a chair, and John Paul sits down while Mr. Perry kneels beside him. The two begin chatting.

"Did he insult you, Cora? Did he insult the WWJD?" John Paul spurts out in his high-pitched Madea voice.

As John Paul continues his Madea impressions, Mr. Perry is unable to contain his laughter. John Paul then informs Mr. Perry that he wants to be in his next movie, and with assurance Mr. Perry tells John Paul he will get him a line.

"One line? Man, I need five or six lines!" he shoots back, still in Madea mode.

Tyler Perry laughs and tells him he will see what he can do.

* * *

It's midafternoon on a Friday, and I get a call from Annette. I can hear the excitement in her voice:

"You're not gonna believe it! I just got an email from Tyler Perry Studios. They want John Paul to be in the new Madea movie."

Her words bring a smile to my face, and I imagine how John Paul will react when he hears the big news. Being the ultimate Tyler Perry fan, John Paul has watched every movie multiple times. His absolute favorite movie character is Mabel "Madea" Simmons. She is a towering, massive, elderly grandmother who is quick to stand up for herself and others. As John Paul says, "Make no bones about it, Madea has a mouth with a meaning."

Annette and I decide not to say anything to John Paul about the Madea movie cameo until we gather all the particulars. It is the hardest thing in the world to have such exciting information and remain silent, but we wanted to make sure everything would work out before sharing the news with John Paul.

Once everything is confirmed, we can finally share the news with him. Not only is he going to have a cameo in the new Madea movie but he is also getting the star treatment while there! A limo picks us up to drive us to the airport. Our seats on the plane have been reserved in first class. Even on the plane John Paul is singled out by the pilot and flight attendants who share his story with the other passengers before takeoff.

As the pilot announces that our plane is first in line for takeoff, John Paul grips the seat, revealing his fear of flying. I hear Annette speak to him: "John Paul, don't worry, it's a beautiful day for flying. Everything is going to be fine. Don't worry. Just think, you are going to meet Tyler Perry again."

John Paul's eyebrows raise slightly, "Tyler Perry? For all I know, I might be going to meet Jesus."

Once in Atlanta the experience of a lifetime continues. John Paul may not like to fly, but he loves to travel and is always thrilled to stay in new hotels and eat out at different restaurants. We check into the hotel booked for us and take the elevator up to the seventeenth floor. Annette opens the door, and John Paul enters the room.

"Wow! Are you kidding me?" He glances back at us as he moves toward the floor-to-ceiling windows displaying a view of Atlanta. "Two bedrooms, two full bathrooms, a living room, three flat screen televisions, computer, and full kitchen...." He pauses, taking everything in. "I can hang with this!"

The next morning we are up bright and early. A van comes to pick us up and take us to the movie set. As we head to downtown Atlanta, it is cold and still dark outside. The driver stops in front of a large glass building, the International Airport. Annette looks stunned, saying, "All the times I've been to Atlanta I never knew there was an airport downtown."

John Paul and I share a glance. "There isn't an airport downtown. It's a movie set," explains John Paul. "Mom, I think you may be having a blonde moment."

The star treatment doesn't stop once we are on set. John Paul receives his own luxury trailer, which is definitely for one of the stars in the movie, but for the day it is all John Paul's. He got to spend time scoping out the bedroom, bathroom, and kitchen—always in search of food—before sitting down to read over his script. Although I am sure this day will forever be etched in my son's memory, Annette takes numerous pictures so he can vividly remember this experience.

I watch while John Paul is escorted to the place where his cameo will take place. I can only imagine how much this means to him. I know how much it means to me and Annette to see the excitement and joy on his face. I remember when Annette told me about the promise Tyler Perry made to John Paul. Now we get to see John Paul's dream become a reality.

It is a blessing to have a person of Tyler Perry's caliber follow through on a promise, especially with such compassion and attention to each detail. For the majority of John Paul's life there have been obstacles. Not every day has unfolded as smoothly or as fantastically as this one. Most of the time, it seems the odds aren't in his favor and there is some struggle or obstacle to overcome.

But there are no obstacles in sight today. John Paul is playing an airline passenger going through security near Madea. He and the actor playing his father stroll through the sequences of his cameo. The director stops as Tyler Perry—in full Madea garb—walks on set. Madea causes a stir in her pink Sunday go-to-church suit, but she's focused on just one person.

Madea walks right up to John Paul, gives him a huge hug, and greets him in her trademark Madea accent, "Hi John Paul! How's it going, baby?"

The smile on John Paul's face is priceless. There is nothing that can equal the joy I feel seeing my son so happy and ecstatic. There is no greater joy than seeing that kind of happiness in the eyes of your child.

Filming continues. All on set—myself included—become absorbed in Madea. It is difficult to suppress our laughter as Madea runs through her scene. I watch John Paul as he tries to contain his laughter while hearing Madea shoot off one-liners and watching her shenanigans live. John Paul is totally immersed in every aspect of this special day. He rubs elbows with fellow actors Eugene Levy and Romeo Miller, and is not at all uncomfortable with his new "movie-star" persona.

While not all of John Paul's days are quite this perfect, this is one trip that will stay with John Paul forever.

Chapter 4

Growing Up

From Annette

Derek and I realized early on that John Paul's life wouldn't be destined for "normalcy." We both knew, however, that his life, still a gift, should be lived as fully as he was able. When he was young we were able to control his environment and surroundings, but as he gets older it becomes more difficult to protect him the way we'd like. It isn't that John Paul makes things difficult for us. In fact, John Paul is an old soul, wise beyond his years. Once a decision is explained to him, he usually accepts it instead of fighting it, a virtue I wish I had. The challenge comes from little, everyday occurrences.

John Paul can't have salt in his diet, which seems insignificant compared to the other obstacles and physical limitations, but it's not. Controlling his salt intake when he was little was easy, but as John Paul gets older it becomes more difficult. There are so many little things we take for granted that John Paul has to approach with caution, such as those indulgence foods we eat like bread, chips, cookies, pizza. All of these foods have salt.

We have found ways for John Paul to indulge in some of these things. We found a bakery that makes salt-free bread and pizza dough. When you know where to look, there are more salt-free items readily available in stores. We even found a pizza place that will make a salt-free pizza.

The chef there knows John Paul, and when we come in he prepares a pizza with no-salt pizza dough, no-sodium tomato sauce, and low-sodium cheese. Then it's delivered to our table just like everyone else's. It might not seem like much, but being able to have this normal experience of going out and indulging in pizza means just as much as all the once-in-a-lifetime experiences.

Chapter 5

From Annette

Throughout John Paul's life, Derek and I have gotten pressure from others about why we don't let John Paul go certain places, eat certain foods, or do certain things. The questions aren't mean-spirited but come from outsiders unfamiliar with John Paul's situation. I'm sure there are times when John Paul feels like he's on the outside looking in, but we try to compensate in other ways.

We've worked to create opportunities for John Paul to meet and mingle with the celebrities he admires. These experiences are bright spots in his memory, but it is also the kindness of our community that has helped John Paul be and feel like he is a part of it, just like at the pizza restaurant. The compassion of friends and acquaintances has gone beyond our wildest expectations.

When he was young it was easier but now, while hanging with Mom and Dad is still OK, he longs to interact with young adults his own age. Not too long ago, he started attending the young-adult ministry at our church. The interaction this group provides has already made an impact on his life. These weekly meetings have not only provided him with spiritual development but also real-life experience. The other young adults in the group have embraced John Paul. In their eyes he is not different; he's one of them. Not only is he a part of the meetings but he also gets invited to go to the movies and dinner. He and his friends text daily, just like any other group of friends. Can you imagine how good this simple, everyday inclusion makes my son feel?

John Paul is different, although I prefer to use the word unique. There are those who notice his uniqueness and ask questions: "*Really, he's twenty years old? He looks ten!"* They are unable to see his scars or hear the story that explains why he is so small and why he isn't exactly like other twenty-year-old men. I know this is the hardest part for John Paul. Every time he is questioned, I feel the pain any mother would feel when she knows her child is hurting.

John Paul has been writing in a journal for years and shared those entries with me for this book. As I was reading through, I noticed that in March 2010 he wrote:

> *I am happy but sad for being short. This will not stop me from playing golf and doing what I want in life.*

John Paul will always have to live with the side effects of his disability and the many obstacles that come with it. Through his journal writings, however, he has been able to take possession of his uniqueness and the realization that it will not define him or hold him back.

In November 2011, John Paul writes:

> *This cross that I'm carrying may be heavy, but I'm not worried about what's ahead. I think about the passion of Christ and his death. Like Isaiah 53:5 says, "by his wounds we were healed." By Jesus' wounds my wounds are healed. I must move forward and let my love of Jesus take control of my life.*

Chapter 6

Chance Encounters

I have a disabled sticker for my car. I'd much rather have a healthy child who did not have to go through countless surgeries and setbacks than a sticker for my car that lets us park close, but that wasn't a choice I was able to make.

I am used to "the looks" John Paul and I get from people when we get out of the car. Neither one of us looks disabled to the outside world, but outward appearances can be deceiving. It is important to remember that a person does not have to be in a wheelchair to be disabled, but not everyone understands this.

This particular Friday night, Annette, John Paul, and I are going to our favorite pizza restaurant. I drop Annette at the front to get a seat while John Paul and I park the car. There is a woman sitting outside the restaurant. She watches me park in the disabled space, and when we walk by she mumbles something under her breath. I ignore her, not sure who she's talking to and not wanting to start anything unnecessarily. Then she speaks louder, causing others to turn and take notice, "You need to move your car. You're not handicapped."

I cannot believe it. "Excuse me?"

"Everyone can clearly see you are not handicapped, so you need to move your car."

John Paul tugs at my arm. "Daddy, what's wrong?"

I do not want John Paul to get upset. I tell him not to worry and that everything is fine, but this woman's attitude is relentless. She continues to harass us as we walk past her. John Paul grips my hand. I use my body as a barrier between him and the woman.

"Why is she mad at us?" His bottom lip begins to quiver.

Now I'm mad. This ignorant and meddlesome woman has upset my son. I open the restaurant door and let John Paul in to join Annette before I go back out to confront her.

"I would appreciate it if you would kindly mind your own business," I tell her.

Everyone standing outside is eavesdropping on the conversation. Even the people inside have started to take notice. I speak loud enough so that everyone can hear. I do not want any further confusion about "the sticker," plus a little education may help others who hastily draw conclusions before knowing the facts.

"A disability is not always something that is visible. A person can be disabled without being in a wheelchair or walking with a cane. I have a sticker because my son has a serious heart problem. Trust me, I would much rather have a healthy child than a sticker that affords me special parking privileges. You should consider others' feelings and think before you speak."

The lady huffs. She couldn't care less, expressing no remorse for her actions. Needless emotional pain was inflicted on my family that night. For days, John Paul inquired why the woman was so mean.

That's a hard question to answer.

Chapter 7

From Annette

Not all of our experiences with strangers out in the world have been negative. Most of the time, people find ways to bond with John Paul, and his unique personality leaves a lasting impression. During a trip to Sears, John Paul and I are waiting on our sales associate, Diane. She knows a little about John Paul's condition and tells us we might like to talk to another one of her customers, Cheryl, who had been through something traumatic recently.

In then talking with Cheryl, I tell her about John Paul's condition. Once she realizes his age, size, and the fact that he has just started college, she instantly connects with his feelings. She talks about how difficult it must be to enter a classroom for the first time, especially because of John Paul's size and the looks and curiosity of his classmates. John Paul is surprised that someone he just met could recognize and identify with that aspect of his disability so quickly. They continue talking, and she tells us that she used to work for IBM.

When she mentions IBM, John Paul is immediately captivated. He loves computers. She refers to the old system, the IBM 360, and that really starts the conversation flowing. She can't believe John Paul knows anything about the old system. I go to the register to complete our purchase, and John Paul stays with Cheryl chatting away like they've been friends for ages.

Diane tells me that Cheryl recently lost her husband and has had a difficult time getting through that loss. Seeing her and John Paul happily engrossed in conversation makes me smile. Sometimes something as simple as a conversation can be therapeutic. But it is I and John Paul who are going to get the most "therapy" from this encounter.

Cheryl approaches me and asks if we could all go to the Apple Store after we finish at Sears. She tells me it won't take long. She wants to buy John Paul an iPad. My immediate response is to thank her for her offer, but John Paul can't possibly accept that kind of gift.

She argues that because John Paul is in college now, having an Apple computer might be beneficial to him. Of course, now that John Paul has wind of the conversation his eyes light up. It's always been his dream to have an Apple computer, but Derek and I have never been able to afford one. Now someone we've just met is offering to buy him one.

Cheryl continues by saying that she wants to "pay it forward." Her husband had always been generous and good to her. She could hear his voice telling her to do this. I am in awe. Nothing like this has ever happened before, and I'm torn about what to do with her offer. John Paul is pleading with excitement. Maybe this is meant to be. I believe God places us where we're supposed to be. Maybe there's a reason John Paul and Cheryl were placed together.

Ecstatic doesn't begin to describe the level of John Paul's excitement. Every trip we'd ever made to the mall included a trip to the Apple Store, but he'd never been able to buy anything. Today is different. As he enters the store with his new friend, he has a purpose. His dream of owning an Apple computer was about to come true.

John Paul walks around the store with Cheryl, saying, "Are you sure this isn't a dream? Pinch me to let me know this is for real!"

I'm finding it even more difficult to express my sincere gratitude.

After getting home and spending the evening setting up John Paul's new computer, I find it as hard to go to sleep as he does. But I'm sleepless for a different reason. I just can't get over this wonderful woman's actions. I can't get what she did off my mind. How could I begin to repay such a generous gift?

Then I think about what John Paul said to his benefactor as they parted ways: "Never in my wildest dreams did I think our conversation would lead me to getting a new Apple computer. All I was hoping for was a friendship."

Chapter 8

From Annette

Because of John Paul, I have encountered the kind of people who touch the very depths of your being. These everyday saints, ordinary people who during their lifetime touch the world in an extraordinary way, have made a true impact. Such people have included the doctors and nurses who cared for John Paul, as well as people around the world who may never meet him but have encompassed him in prayer. Through our son we have entered into a deeper communion with God, our community, and those around the world.

When John Paul was born, I was frightened. I had been strong and upbeat during the pregnancy, but then I was face to face with my beautiful son and his life-threatening condition. I had known all along about the outcome dictated by specialists, but I did not believe it would be my son's fate. I believed faith, not fate, would be John Paul's compass into and throughout life.

It's amazing how God works. He sent a special woman into my life to help settle my anxious feelings. I will never forget our first encounter. Kathy Brown came bouncing to John Paul's bedside and introduced herself. Her smile added a brightness to the dimly lit PICU, and her eyes emitted kindness.

Kathy was John Paul's primary care nurse from day one and my nurturer from then on as well. While making sure John Paul received the best care possible, she also sprinkled some happiness into each of the long, timeless days in the hospital by sharing her family anecdotes and catch phrases, like "*have gas will travel.*" Whether Kathy's shift was day or night, she was there for us unconditionally. It wasn't just our family that benefited from her exceptional caregiving abilities, but all the families who were her patients.

Her guardianship, or perhaps guardian-angelship, didn't stop once our family exited the hospital. Kathy made routine visits to our house and called frequently to make sure all was going well.

To ensure John Paul was in the best of health, we moved to a warmer climate, which meant losing the close connections we'd made in North Carolina. Katie and I stayed in touch for a while, but as the years passed we slowly started to lose contact.

We did, however, still keep in touch through social media. We shared updates on our families and talked about John Paul's progress. Recently, I noticed Kathy had stopped posting and that's when I found out the devastating news that our friend had passed away.

The tender loving care Kathy showered on all her patients and their families was immense. Kathy was a down-to-earth, ordinary person, but to those she met and touched in her special way, she was extraordinary. She has truly impacted all of our lives, and her legacy will not be forgotten.

Chapter 9

Annette has a way about her. It's kind of unexplainable, but when she wants to contact someone who has inspired John Paul, she somehow accomplishes the task. Maybe it's that Southern drawl or unassuming manner, but whatever it is, over the years she usually succeeds. One of her first contacts was made shortly after John Paul's third-stage surgery. We were in North Carolina, staying with her parents, so we could be near the hospital and doctors while John Paul recovered.

I remember one afternoon she goes into the bedroom with the phone in her hand saying she has to make a call. About thirty minutes later she comes out with a smile on her face. "I just spoke to Jerry Bledsoe!" she exclaims.

Author Jerry Bledsoe lives in North Carolina and is known for several true-crime titles as well as some endearing books about giving, love, and friendship. Annette has shared John Paul's story and his will to survive with him. Jerry immediately asks about the possibility of us writing a book to share our son's inspiring story. Although Annette and I talked about it, we pushed that thought into the background. Right now we know that our focus needs to be on John Paul and his health.

As John Paul continues to grow and thrive, friends and family begin to bring up the idea of a book again. They all think John Paul and his story radiate hope—from his smile to his kindness and appreciation of being able to live life to the fullest—and that we should write the story of his incredible and miraculous life.

I am a little hesitant at first. I don't want to dwell on the past. I want to look to the future. But the more the idea is discussed the more I realize this story could be beneficial—even inspirational—to others. I remembered the vow I'd made in the hospital about sharing John Paul's story. I knew it was a story we would have to tell.

I decide to put my thoughts on paper and began drafting the first chapter. The words surge onto the page as if my hand can't keep pace with my thoughts. Memories, circumstances, and everything that I'd suppressed in the back of my mind comes out. By writing John Paul's story, I travel that journey again. This time, however, I am not in the moment. I am not constantly on edge and having to make critical decisions, wondering if my son will survive. I am able to think and reflect on everything we'd experienced during this critical time. I am able to meditate on the numerous miracles through which God has blessed Annette, John Paul, and me.

Once the manuscript is finished, I hand it over to Annette to read. Sometimes I watch her as she reads to see how she reacts to certain sections, the emotions, and the way I've written John Paul's story. Naturally, her personal connection makes her more emotional than the average reader, but her demeanor serves as a gauge to how others might be moved by John Paul's story. This book is a heartfelt love letter to my son, sharing his strength and courage with anyone who might stumble across it.

A dear priest, who since has passed away, and I talk about John Paul and the manuscript. I want a seasoned author to take a look at it and maybe even endorse it. We can use that endorsement as a way to let more people know about John Paul's story. But I know my chances of getting the book to someone like that are slim. The priest tells me I should contact a member of his parish—James Patterson. I think there is no way he'll be willing to look at this manuscript, let alone even want to get in touch with us. The priest encourages me, however, and I know with God's hand at work anything is possible.

I pass the suggestion along to Annette and watch as she grabs the phone, goes to our room, and shuts the door. She is in the room for about ten minutes before coming out with an enormous smile on her face.

"I can't believe that I just called James Patterson's house! Can you believe it?"

I stand dumbfounded, wondering how she'd managed to get James Patterson's home phone number, but I don't question. She explains, with a hint of excitement, that she had just called James Patterson's house and his wife answered the phone. She told her a little bit about John Paul and his amazing story before mentioning the manuscript. Mrs. Patterson put

Annette through to James' personal assistant who agreed to pass our book on to him.

Needless to say, we send the manuscript that very day. It doesn't take long before we receive a response from his personal assistant:

Hello Annette:

Mr. Patterson has provided a quote for the book. It is:

"This is a touching and uplifting true story about a boy named John Paul, who has half a heart but who lives with more heart and soul than just about any kid you will ever meet. John Paul rocks, and so does this book."

We wish you the very best of luck with the book.

Chapter 10

Annette and I had made the decision together to not tell John Paul about the full extent of his disability and illness. We worried that hearing the story all at once with all the details would be too overwhelming and too all-consuming for him. We wanted to give John Paul the best chance at living his life to the fullest without those "what ifs" hanging over his head.

He certainly wasn't oblivious to his condition. John Paul has always known he has a heart condition, which meant that he couldn't go to school like other kids his age, or eat the same foods or participate in the same sports. We didn't tell him that he wasn't supposed to live beyond birth. We didn't explain about the three major surgeries, the complications, or what could go wrong. We wanted to protect John Paul. But we weren't able to keep those details from him forever.

John Paul loves golf, a sport perfect for him with his condition. God has also blessed John Paul with a talent for the sport. Because of his love for golf he is asked to be the standard bearer at the 2009 Honda Classic. When Annette and I agree to this, we do not realize that it will be a turning point for our son. John Paul is paired with Erik Compton, a PGA Tour player and two-time heart-transplant recipient. When the media finds out the incredible heart link between Erik and John Paul they lock onto the story.

These interviewers question me about John Paul and his condition. They ask me to explain hypoplastic left heart syndrome. I give them the details of John Paul's condition and all the obstacles he'd had to overcome. I don't realize John Paul is by my side, listening to every word, until I feel his hand reach for mine. I look down, our eyes meet, and my stomach drops. Then a smile crosses his face and he squeezes my hand, and I know he is OK.

On the way home Annette and I ask him if he has any questions about the facts that came out that day. He ponders for a few minutes, "No, I'm good."

Through a round of golf John Paul not only learned a great deal more about his disability but also realized, by watching and talking to Erik, that there were others in the world who have disabilities. Just like with so many other things, John Paul surprises us with what he can accept. He will be OK.

Chapter 11

John Paul constantly pulls at his mom's ear about his desire to meet Tiger Woods. I often hear Annette pacify him by saying *"maybe someday,"* but in our private conversations we discuss how remote the possibility is that this will happen. In private, Annette is trying, without much luck, every avenue to make John Paul's dream come true.

Thursday morning after Mass, we are talking to a good friend about the Arnold Palmer Invitational, which is being played in Orlando. Back in the car, I nonchalantly mention to Annette that Tiger is playing the tournament and maybe a tournament official could help John Paul meet Tiger. It only takes minutes for Annette to get started.

Within twenty minutes of leaving a message for the tournament director, the phone rings.

"I spoke to the tournament director's assistant, Tiffany. She wants us to plan to come to the tournament tomorrow morning early and she will meet us there. She said she can't promise, but she is going to try her best to get John Paul to meet Tiger."

We walk back into the kitchen, where John Paul is eating breakfast. Annette shares the news with John Paul, who jumps out of his chair and does a Tiger fist pump.

Before the sun rises, we are out at the putting green watching the professionals putt under the bright florescent lights. Tiffany comes and introduces herself and takes us inside the tournament offices. John Paul is in awe. He quickly notices a large photo on the wall of Tiger holding the trophy from his previous win. "That would look really cool on my wall," he says.

Tiffany shows us around and then explains that we will go with the tournament director to the first tee and watch Tiger tee off. Then we can walk along with the crowd and watch him play. After the round, we will meet Tiffany on the practice tee and hopefully at that time John Paul can meet Tiger.

We are ushered to a special vantage point on the first tee from which we watch Tiger tee his first drive and begin following his round. The crowd is astounding and it's hard to see, so we walk a couple of holes ahead and wait at the greens. When Tiger exits the green, he does something very unusual. He looks at John Paul and says, "Hey kid, think quick." Then he tosses John Paul his ball. The galley cheers in awe, knowing that this is a rarity for Tiger.

"Thank goodness I caught it!" John Paul says, admiring the ball.

After the round, Tiffany and the tournament manager lead John Paul to the media room, where he is able to watch as Tiger answers questions. Afterward Tiger is introduced to John Paul, and the two talk, take pictures, and Tiger signs John Paul's cap and a few other collectibles.

That Christmas, John Paul receives a new collector's item. In the box from Tiffany is the large picture of Tiger that had been on the wall at the Arnold Palmer Invitational, but as John Paul reaches deeper into the box he finds something else: "Hey, look at this! Tiger signed this picture of us!"

"You are one lucky boy, John Paul," I say.

"You're right, Dad. I am very lucky."

Chapter 12

John Paul loves football, both American and European. These sports require too much energy and contact for John Paul to play, but it doesn't stop him from watching. Growing up across the pond, soccer was a huge part of my life and even today I give my support to Manchester United. Naturally, I've passed on that passion to John Paul who also enthusiastically supports Man United. Like any other superstitious sports fan, John Paul has his own routine any time the Red Devils play. He wears the same soccer jersey no matter if it's dirty or clean and stands by the television cheering as loud as he can. He immerses himself in the Manchester United team spirit, with posters of yesteryear heroes and today's stars plastered on his walls. When he was younger, his goal was to make the team. Most boys could turn those dreams into a more realistic goal by playing for a local or school team, but John Paul has to settle for kicking the ball around and attempting to score against me.

John Paul possesses that same excitement for the NFL. He is a big fan of the San Francisco 49ers and Baltimore Ravens. He is also a big fan of Michael Clayton.

I actually have the pleasure of meeting Michael Clayton, the wide receiver for the Tampa Bay Bucs. Our conversation revolves around John Paul and his love of football. The next home game, Michael organizes tickets for us to come and watch him play.

This is John Paul's first time going to an NFL game, and he cannot contain his excitement walking into the stadium. We get an escort to our awesome seats, first row right in the end zone. Even Annette and I are thrilled with the experience, and John Paul is especially happy chatting with the cheerleaders as they walk pass. There are so many highlights: the singing of the national anthem, the flyover by the military jets, and the loud cannon shots from the pirate ship at each Tampa Bay score.

The real high spot, though, is when the Bucs edge toward the end zone where we are seated. We watch as Michael runs toward the end zone. The quarterback drops back to throw, and the ball drops into Michael's arms.

Touchdown!

Then Michael runs toward us. I nudge John Paul, and he leans over the rail where Michael reaches to give him a high five. For that moment, John Paul isn't on the sidelines. He is in front of 65,000 people. He is part of the team.

Michael has continued to be an amazing friend to John Paul, also arranging for him to come watch the Tampa Bay Bucs play the San Francisco 49ers in style. Michael didn't stop there. He knows that John Paul loves Manchester United, and it just so happens that the owner of the Bucs, the Glazer family, also owns Manchester United. Michael arranges it so that John Paul gets the surprise of his life, all the memorabilia imaginable from his favorite team, including a signed Man United jersey from his favorite player, Wayne Rooney.

Chapter 13

From Annette

John Paul has become adept at celebrity sightings. A few years ago John Paul and I receive tickets to a movie sneak preview in downtown West Palm Beach. Derek is out of town, so we decide to make an evening of the event and go for dinner at the Cheesecake Factory. The restaurant is bustling. Michael Jackson just left, which is quite a star sighting for that area. John Paul questions the waiter, who fills him in on the scoop.

"By the way, I hear Chris Tucker from *Rush Hour* is also at City Place," the waiter tells John Paul. This sends John Paul over the top. Michael Jackson might be the king of pop, but John Paul is a movie buff and an avid fan of Chris Tucker and the *Rush Hour* movies.

John Paul exclaims, "Where is he?!"

The waiter tells John Paul he heard that Chris Tucker is at the movie theater. Normally a slow eater, John Paul gobbles up his food and exclaims he's ready to go to the movie! The waiter brings the bill and an update. Michael Jackson has been sighted at Barnes & Noble.

"John Paul," I say, "we have to go to Barnes & Noble. This is a once-in-a-lifetime chance to meet Michael Jackson."

"Mom, I want to go see Chris Tucker."

"We still have plenty of time," I respond. "Let's go and see if we can see Michael Jackson, and we'll go straight to the movie from there."

John Paul agrees reluctantly. At Barnes & Noble, the music section is closed, allowing Michael Jackson to shop alone. John Paul is now thrilled and wants to meet him, and John Paul is not shy. He sneaks into the music section and goes directly up to Michael Jackson, "Excuse me, do you have the *Pearl Harbor* video?"

Michael Jackson looks at his bodyguard and laughs, "The kid thinks I work here."

The bodyguard is ready to escort John Paul out, but Michael Jackson stops him. He proceeds to scan the store, John Paul at his side, looking for *Pearl Harbor*. When he finds it, he hands it to John Paul and they walk over toward me.

Michael Jackson motions for me to come over to him, "Your son wants this *Pearl Harbor* video."

I graciously thank him for helping John Paul and ask for an autograph. I search through my purse, but all I can find is my Cheesecake Factory receipt and my eyeliner pencil. I hand them both to him and he laughs.

"You want me to sign with an eyeliner pencil?"

By now the crowd notices that he is signing autographs and start pushing their way toward him with things to sign. He uses the eyeliner pencil to sign our receipt, hands it back to me, smiles at John Paul, and then moves through the crowd with his bodyguard to exit the store.

With that star sighting over, John Paul is ready to move on to the next one, "Come on, Mom, we got to hurry. We got to get to the movie theater."

At the theater, the attendant explains that the movie is full and no one else is allowed in. Needless to say, John Paul is disappointed. The attendant overhears John Paul say he wants to meet Chris Tucker and informs us that Chris Tucker is in the movie showing we were supposed to see. That's all John Paul needs to hear. We have to sit and wait. Thirty minutes pass, then forty-five.

"John Paul, it's getting late," I finally say. "The movie will not be out for another forty-five minutes. We really need to go. You already met Michael Jackson."

Call it fate, destiny, whatever you want, but just as we start to leave I see someone walk out of the theater.

"Mom, that's Chris Tucker!"

The man turns around, catches a glimpse of John Paul, smiles, and says, "Hey there, little man."

The two carry on a conversation for ten minutes talking about *Rush Hour*. He is amazed that John Paul knows all the one-liners. John Paul asks for his autograph, and when he can't find anything for Chris Tucker to sign points to his new white Air Jordans. Chris Tucker, who thankfully has his own pen, gets down on his hands and knees to sign my son's shoes: "*Love, Chris Tucker.*"

I thank him for being so nice and explain a little about John Paul's condition. He takes out a card, writes his and his agent's home numbers on it, and looks at John Paul, "I want you to come to my next movie premiere. You mom has my numbers. We'll stay in touch."

John Paul's eyes light up. He gives Chris a hug and thanks him. As we start to walk away, John Paul turns and adds one more commentary, "By the way, you need to get a new partner. Jackie Chan is getting too old."

"Who do you think my new partner should be?"

John Paul does a karate move and smiles, "Me!"

Chapter 14

Hope

From Annette

Some people start out life in an ordinary or humble manner. For example, Harry Truman, Andrew Jackson, Abe Lincoln, Ronald Reagan, and Barack Obama all came from humble backgrounds, yet they obtained and held the highest office in America, the presidency.

During the 2000 presidential election, John Paul becomes fascinated with the role of the president. Previously, on any given election night, we would have the name of our next president before bedtime. The election night in 2000, however, was not like any other and a decisive winner does not emerge until weeks later. This scenario spikes John Paul's interest, and he decides he wants to meet the president of the United States.

His desire spurs me to begin that quest. I try every avenue I can think of to help him meet President George W. Bush. After countless roadblocks, I do something out of character; I stop trying.

In 2008, John Paul follows the election proceedings and the inauguration of the new president with renewed interest. He makes a comment while watching the inauguration that maybe he can meet the new, history-making president. I explain how hard I had tried before, that I just don't know if meeting the president of the United States is something within our reach. But even while saying these words I know, deep down, I'm not really done trying. I'll do whatever it takes to make John Paul's dream a reality this time.

Motivation steers me into overdrive as I go through the list of who could possibly help John Paul meet the president. I call and email our representatives, but my efforts are in vain until I get in touch with Senator Bill Nelson's office. When the staff hears John Paul's story, they say that they will try their best to facilitate a meeting. Now we have to exercise the virtue of patience.

In early 2011, I receive an email from the office of Senator Nelson inviting John Paul to join himself and President Obama at a reception at the Fontainebleau in Miami Beach. It takes longer than I originally anticipated, but we are able to make another of John Paul's dreams come true.

Chapter 15

Many people relate to our family's story because of what their children or family members are going or have gone through. It isn't necessarily that people have a condition resembling John Paul's, but rather the similar experience of dealing with a sick loved one, a hardship, or desperation when hope seemed nonexistent.

It amazes me how John Paul always touches the hearts of those who hear his story. People question how it is possible for someone to live with half a heart. "It's a miracle" is our standard response. That's the only way to describe it. The left side of the heart is vital because it takes the blood to all parts of the body and the right side takes the blood to the lungs. Because the left side of John Paul's heart is dead, the "plumbing" has been reconstructed and rerouted so that the right ventricle does the work of both sides of the heart. When we tell this story people listen, engrossed in John Paul's miracle.

During a recent book signing, a boy, about age fifteen, enters. He proceeds to the front of the line, ignoring the others waiting. The teenager walks with a slight limp, and his right arm appears paralyzed and remains stationary by his side. He picks up a copy of the book with his left hand and examines the cover and contents. I don't say anything, continuing to sign books while he browses through the copy. Finally, he acknowledges me, lays the book back on the table, and says he will be right back.

Not long afterward a woman, looking tired and stressed, follows the boy to the front of the line. She explains to me that the boy is her son, and while he really wants a copy of the book, they can't afford it right now. I pick up a copy of *Heart of a Lion*, sign it, and ask Annette to pay for the book.

I watch as tears form in the woman's eyes: "My son just got out of the hospital this morning. It has been a difficult ordeal. He's been in there for two months and all he wanted to do was stop by the bookstore on our way home. It's really amazing how he was destined to be here and how your book captured him. It has been a very long two months, and I think your son's story can help him heal."

She does not elaborate on the circumstances of her son's hospital stay, and I do not ask. That day I felt my purpose was to be in that bookstore to share hope through my son's story, especially with that young man and his mother. I could identify with her anguish. I empathized with her, knowing what it's like to be a parent struggling to care for a sick child. While I hope John Paul's story offers her and her family some support, I wish I could have done more to help.

Chapter 16

A few years ago, John Paul and I have the pleasure of witnessing a truly remarkable event. Florida's governor at the time was Charlie Crist, one of the individuals on John Paul's list of people he wanted to meet. Annette arranges for a meeting with the governor. We meet Governor Crist at Biscayne National Park in southern Florida. The park is home to Biscayne Bay and offshore barrier reefs that the park preserves. As we pull into the parking area, John Paul noticed a caravan of media trucks and reporters standing poised and ready to relate the story of interest to their viewers. Individuals from the Dolphin Research Center, along with the Miami Sea Aquarium and the Florida Wildlife Commission, were busy unloading Patsy, a thousand-pound manatee, out of a truck. A few weeks earlier, Patsy was rescued from a fishing line entanglement that had cut into her flipper. Fortunately for Patsy, she had been nursed back to health and was now healthy enough to be released. The reason that her release has been so carefully calculated is because Patsy is expecting a calf. It is important for her to give birth in the wild, in her own ecosystem.

There are a number of people standing and chatting while awaiting the governor's arrival. A procession of black SUVs arrive, and within minutes Governor Crist exits one. John Paul waits patiently while the governor meets and greets the few who have been given clearance to be present. As his path brings him closer, a big smile lights up John Paul's face. Approaching John Paul, the governor extends his hand for a firm handshake and then proceeds to embrace my son. The two speak for a few minutes, talking about where John Paul lives, his homeschooling, and his interests. After taking a few photos, Governor Crist asks if John Paul is ready for the big release. Enthusiastically, John Paul nods, and the two walk toward the bay.

Not only does John Paul get to meet another one of his inspirations but we also get to be a part of this miraculous event.

Life Lessons

> *We've had so many amazing experiences with John Paul,*
> *but some of the best have been those small, everyday*
> *experiences of just having him in our life. That's what we*
> *want to capture with these short snapshots.*

Chapter 17

Fashion Is in the Eye of the Wearer

John Paul had emergency brain surgery at four years old. After that surgery, he sports a bright yellow bumblebee helmet from the time he wakes up in the morning to the time he goes to bed. The helmet probably isn't a necessity, but Annette and I are cautious because we don't want him to stumble and hit his head.

He turns that yellow bumblebee helmet into his trademark look for the rest of the year. In fact, he won't go anywhere without it by choice!

Chapter 18

Life With *John Paul Can Be Hard;* *Life* Without *Him Would Be Impossible*

As part of my mission to share John Paul's story of hope, I do speaking engagements. After sharing John Paul's story with the students at the IDEAL School in Royal Palm Beach, Florida, I asked if anyone had any questions. A young girl raises her hand and asks, "What would life be like without John Paul in it?"

This questions stuns me. I am motionless for a few seconds as I think about the answer to that question. It's one that hits deep. I can't imagine living my life without John Paul. Keeping John Paul safe and healthy is the reason that Annette and I are so protective, and why we've kept John Paul so sheltered.

We can't imagine a life without him.

Chapter 19

Mountain Life

From Annette

John Paul loves the mountains of North Carolina and, although a sensitivity to elevation is another side effect of John Paul's condition, the elevation there has never seemed to bother him. He's able to experience all the beauty those mountains hold. We have traveled along the Blue Ridge Parkway, taken small hikes on the trails, and gazed at the scenery of rolling mountains from the overlooks.

Grandfather Mountain in Linville, North Carolina, is one of John Paul's favorite attractions. When looking at the mountain, the shape of the trees and rocks forms a profile of a man's face, hence the name Grandfather Mountain. The road leading up to the peak provides views of the rolling hills, but it's the Mile High Swinging Bridge that commands the most breathtaking views layered with the suspense of a moving bridge. His favorite time of year is fall, when the leaves are bright and colorful. We try to go to the mountains every two years, and John Paul really settles in, absorbing the culture of the laid-back, generous people and the true Southern foods. He often mentions that life seems easier there and, for some reason, mountain food just tastes better. Maybe I'm biased, being from the mountains myself, but I have to agree with him 100 percent.

Chapter 20

We All Have Scars

Being a parent is a gift. Having a child unearths an innate unconditional love, a love that encourages us to surround our child with a protective shield. Being a parent of a child with a disability heightens that instinct. For years I was able to balance John Paul's life with a sense of normalcy. As he grew older, however, it became obvious that John Paul would have questions. Why was there a scar that marked the length of his chest? What was the scar etched in his hairline? How did he get all the other scars on his body? Why was his left leg smaller than his right, and why did he walk with a limp?

These would be difficult questions to answer. Not difficult in the sense that I did not know the answer, but that I had lived through these agonizing events and would have to live through them again to explain those scars to John Paul.

Of all the scars, the one down the middle of his chest is by far the most obvious and the one my son will notice every day of his life. It will be a constant reminder of his condition, but also a tribute to the miracle of his life. The amazing thing is that John Paul is now twenty years old and to this day has never inquired about this scar. To a certain extent, I believe that John Paul has always had wisdom beyond his years and is able to accept himself without question.

Those scars have become such a part of who he is that he doesn't need to know who he would be without them.

Chapter 21

Our Father's Love Is All-Encompassing

John Paul and I are on the beach with a couple of friends and their children. The children were running around in the bright sunlight, kicking a soccer ball and enjoying themselves. John Paul wants to be a part of their game. I can see him pleading with me through his eyes. The whole situation causes me to shake with anguish.

I question: *Why can't he just be normal? Why can't he have a natural life, playing and enjoying time with his friends?*

I would absolutely give my life for that. Inside I am crying, but I don't want John Paul to know. I hug him and let him know all will be OK. I lean over and encompass John Paul in my arms. No words need to be spoken. I do not realize it at the time, but one of our friends captures this powerful moment with a photo.

This photo embodies the unconditional bond that John Paul and I share. The bond knows no boundaries, a shadow of God's unconditional, loving embrace that encompasses us all.

Chapter 22

The Future

I am constantly reminded that each moment with John Paul is precious. My top priority in life is that my son remains healthy. Of all the dreams and aspirations I have for John Paul, down deep my only desire is that he is here on this earth at least one day longer than I am. I can't imagine living life without my son. Even now I continuously ask others to pray for John Paul, because I believe that without those prayers he wouldn't be here today.

Annette and I have tried to nourish John Paul with love, compassion, understanding, and a devotion to God through our faith. As with any parent, when it comes time to let go and let your child venture into the world, you can only hope that you have instilled within them the tools they will need to face their new beginning.

As I have said many times, John Paul is here for a reason. Early in John Paul's life, Annette and I spoke about the possibility of our son becoming a priest. We never mentioned this to him because we wanted him to discover that calling for himself. If it really was his calling it had to come from God, not Mom and Dad. At a young age, John Paul did start contemplating this call and made it known to us. Knowing he felt this call on his own, we nourish it the best we can.

John Paul recently started college. You can't imagine what a milestone of a day that was for Annette and me! I couldn't help but think back to those early days in Annette's pregnancy when we were told there was no hope for our unborn child. Twenty years later, "our hope" took his first step into adulthood. That step would not have been possible without the grace of God, a grace that will continue to sustain John Paul throughout his life.

From Annette

John Paul feels called to become a priest, and because he wanted to explore this call further he decides to go to a vocations retreat at a seminary in Miami. He is apprehensive about being away from home for the first time. Naturally, as a mom, I am feeling the same way.

A couple of days before the retreat, John Paul and I are driving to the grocery store and he is beginning to feel a little nervous about being away. He questions me, asking if he should go. I think for a minute, then tell John Paul that he is a special young man and that God gave him the gift of life for a purpose.

Now it is time for him to spread his wings and fly.

IN JOHN PAUL'S WORDS

Chapter 23

Growing up with a heart condition hasn't been easy, especially when it comes to school. At the time, I really didn't understand what was wrong or the extent of my heart condition. I just knew I couldn't be around people when they were sick and that my parents were always focused on keeping me healthy and away from anything contagious.

I also knew that I wanted to be like other kids and go to school. It took a while, but eventually my parents caved and let me attend kindergarten like all the other kids. I loved my teacher and classmates, but then I got sick. That put an end to my school experience.

After that, I had a teacher who came to my house. Mrs. Velente and I got along really well (and are still buddies today). It was hard for me to pick up on things, though, and Mrs. Velente could only tutor me so many hours a week. It was frustrating to be spending all my time working on my lessons, only to feel like I wasn't making progress. I needed a different kind of school, so my parents decided to try homeschooling.

There wasn't much adjusting to being homeschooled because I hadn't spent that long in a classroom. The only real difference I noticed was that instead of a teacher, I had my parents. With my parents as my teachers there was no goofing off. Just because I have a heart condition doesn't mean I can't act like other boys my age. There were plenty of days when I wanted to be lazy and watch TV or play games instead of focusing on school. Those temptations were in my classroom every day. But Mom and Dad were tough; they adhered to a strict schedule and I had to comply.

Of course, as I got older there were times when I wanted to go to school and be in class with people my own age. My parents tried to explain the risks of getting sick and that it wasn't worth taking that chance, but it wasn't easy to accept.

My parents tried to make up for all the experiences I didn't get by giving me different kinds of experiences. I've gotten to travel to many interesting places and even meet some of my favorite celebrities. I have to live with the repercussions of my disability, like not being able to have the "typical" school experience, and again that isn't always easy. Do I wish that I would have been able to go to school like everyone else? Absolutely! I can only imagine the things I missed out on that could only have been experienced in a traditional school setting: sporting events, pep rallies, prom, class pictures, a graduation ceremony, or even just walking down a crowded hallway to get to class. Still, there will always be things in life that we have to give up or don't get to experience for one reason or another, whether it's because of a disability or something else. I've found opportunities to become well rounded in other ways and make new experiences for myself. I think I've turned out pretty good!

Chapter 24

Even though I've missed out on some more traditional school experiences, being homeschooled has given me certain advantages. I love to read and always have. Each book I read allows me to travel through my imagination, and for me that's sometimes the safest way to travel. I don't have to worry about getting sick and can still go to places all over the world. Although homeschooling means a lot of time "traveling" in books, it also means the opportunity to travel in reality.

We were able to travel any time of the year because I could just take my school work with me. That traveling usually became a lesson in itself. Just like other school groups go on field trips to museums, historic sites, or Washington, DC, my parents made it possible for me to go to all these places too. My parents are very cautious about keeping me healthy in everyday situations, so you can imagine the many precautions they take when we travel. I always joke with my mom because I do believe she uses an entire bottle of Lysol to spray each and every hotel room in which we stay. My dad and I always have to leave the room while she sprays, just so we can breathe. She also has a lot of bottles of hand sanitizers when we go on a trip. All these safety measures, though, are well worth the benefits of visiting new and different places.

The museums we visited were the visuals that helped reinforce everything I was learning. My favorites were the National Air and Space Museum, and the American History and Natural History museums. I was fascinated by all the airplanes that I saw suspended from the museum ceilings. Being from North Carolina, my parents told me a great deal about the Wright brothers. It was amazing to see their plane in person, not to mention the Spirit of St. Louis! Each museum held something special that

I enjoyed. Not only was it a great experience but I also was able to make it part of my schooling.

Everything I was learning about science and history was presented to me in a visual way. I loved that because I'm a visual person. Dad says that I probably learn best that way because even when I was just a few days old the nurses placed a television in front of my crib. They played Disney sing-alongs to keep my mind occupied, so I wouldn't pull out the IVs and machinery to which I was hooked up. Sometimes though I have learned the most through chance encounters. I love history. Once on a cruise I met an older gentleman who shared his wealth of knowledge on Pearl Harbor and World War II. I sat and spoke with him for hours and learned things that my history book could never bring to life as this man's stories did.

I like to think that I didn't lose out on any school experiences. Instead, I just traded the traditional ones for ones unique to me.

Chapter 25

I love people. I love to talk, laugh, and socialize. With my heart condition, though, I have not been able to throw myself into the "social scene" like most people my age. I have always been able to socialize with my family and a small group of friends, but now that I've started college I have the opportunity to expand my social circle and experience life in a different way. I'm still aware of everything I need to do to stay healthy. Mom makes sure I have hand sanitizer in my backpack, but being able to be in a college setting and mingle with others is priceless for me.

I never felt like I missed out on anything growing up. My parents made sure of that. The things that I enjoyed growing up, like eating at Outback, going to movies, watching Seinfeld reruns, listening to music, and socializing on Facebook, are still some of my favorite things to do now. Mom and Dad have made my life as normal as possible, but they knew that because of my health there would always be restrictions and I wouldn't be able to socialize in the "normal" way. I guess that's one reason that whenever I mentioned I wanted to meet someone they did their best to make it happen. I have been blessed with being able to meet some of the people I admire most: James Patterson, Jack Nicklaus, Tyler Perry, Tiger Woods, Chris Tucker, Michael Jackson, and my all-time favorite Bond girl, Jane Seymour.

It is only through God and the compassion of others that I have been blessed with all these unique opportunities. It has meant a great deal to me, especially when I wasn't able to have the same everyday experiences as other kids my age.

Chapter 26

Since the 2000 presidential election, I have wanted to meet the president. Mom tried relentlessly, but she always came up empty handed, until she contacted Florida's Senator Nelson and his team make it happen.

I don't think there is a word that expresses the excitement I feel when I hear I am going to meet President Obama. I mean, the president of the United States! Can you believe it? Even after the shock starts to wear off, the reality that I am going to be in the same room with the president still seems unbelievable. The magnitude of the whole occasion really starts to set in when Mom provides our personal information for a background check. I can't help but joke with Mom, telling her not to worry. If she doesn't pass the background check, Dad and I will bring her a souvenir. I mark each and every day off of my calendar until the day arrives.

The hour-long drive to Miami seems endless. When we finally arrive in downtown Miami Beach, we witness first-hand the safety precautions that go into organizing and preparing for the president's arrival. Roads are blocked off, and security personnel are everywhere.

As we entered the Fontainebleau Hotel, we are directed to a large open area and told to stand and wait. Mom likes to arrive early, so we are one of the first parties there. Slowly the space begins to fill up. I look at all the people and begin to wonder if I am really going to meet President Obama, or if I will just see him from a distance among all the other people.

Organizers arrive and begin checking people in and handing out different-colored plastic wristbands. We are grouped in different sections based on the color of our wristbands. The majority of people continue to stand in the large, open area, but we are told to stand at the bottom of the escalators with a small group. Finally, we are escorted up to the escalators and a small room.

Inside the room are tables stacked with food and drink. Meeting the president just got better! I love food. I guess you could say that I'm a food junkie, so whenever food enters the equation I get really happy. I hit the hors d'oeuvres, load my plate, and take a seat at a table to relish my food.

There are fewer than fifty people in our private room. Every time the door opens I hold my breath, hoping it is the president. Senator Bill Nelson approaches our table and introduces himself and his son, Bill Nelson Jr. Standing up to greet him, I realize that not only am I meeting my state senator but also an astronaut who was on the Space Shuttle Columbia. I have to admit that this is pretty cool. I thank him for allowing me to be a part of this day and ask if I can have my picture taken with him.

After meeting Senator Nelson, I am even more anxious to meet the president. I am not good at waiting, so I decide that another trip to the hors d'oeuvres table will help me pass the time.

The chatter inside the room intensifies, and I notice a group of men in suits stationing themselves near a set of doors. Someone says "the President is here." My eyes remain glued to the entrance. The double doors open and in he walks, sporting his trademark smile. It's a magnetic and contagious smile that draws you in, an uplifting smile that makes you feel like he's your friend, a good friend.

President Obama goes to the podium. He has the undivided attention of everyone in the room as he speaks. Afterward, it is finally time for the meet and greet. Mom, Dad, and I walk up to him. He extends his hand toward mine and says, "How are you?" He sounds just like he does on television, and I am in awe.

After shaking hands, he tells me he likes my shirt. Then we're able to take a quick picture. I am impressed about how nice and down to earth he is to me. For a minute it did seem like I was talking to a friend and not the president of the United States.

Chapter 27

My Mom and Dad are very set in their ways when it comes to keeping me healthy, especially during the winter months with all the colds and flu going around. Because of that concern, I hadn't been able to attend many book signing events with my parents. Still, when a book signing comes up in sunny South Florida, only a few minutes from home, I get the go-ahead to attend. Of course, my parents continue to set boundaries for my well-being. I have to fist pump instead of shake hands and continuously use hand sanitizer. These are all rules that I've come to expect. The routine is the same no matter where we go: church, movies, shopping, you name it.

When we arrive at Barnes & Noble, there is a table and two chairs stationed by the entrance. Dad and I take our positions to sign books. Mom has contacted James Patterson's personal assistant to let him know about the book signing. I am hoping that he'll stop by, but Mom explains that he's probably too busy to make it. James Patterson is one of my favorite authors. I especially love his Alex Cross novels, and I was thrilled that he took the time to give such a great endorsement for *Heart of a Lion*.

Even though I want James Patterson to come, I am still shocked to see him walking inside. My dad and I both watch him as he comes our way. He comes to the table where we are signing books and sits down with me. Now trust me, that gets the customer's attention! They could not believe what they were seeing, James Patterson signing our book! How amazing is that?

While signing books James Patterson and I chat. We talk about my friendship with Tyler Perry, who also happened to play Alex Cross in the movie version of James Patterson's Alex Cross. It is a thrill to be able to talk directly to the author of my favorite books, especially while he is signing copies of our book *Heart of a Lion*!

Chapter 28

I do still have one dream that I haven't been able to make come true, to one day meet the pope. Our Holy Father remains at the top of my wish list and, hopefully, one day that dream will become a reality. It isn't just the pope that's on the top of my wish list, though. Of all the places I dream of visiting, Rome is first on my list. To me, it's the ultimate destination. Not only do I want to meet the pope but I also want to go and experience the beauty of the city. Since I was old enough to learn about Pope John Paul II, my namesake, I have always wanted to meet our pope. As I discern becoming a priest, this desire has become even stronger.

I love the movie *The Agony and the Ecstasy,* which tells the story of Michelangelo as he painted the Sistine Chapel's ceiling. Just seeing these masterpieces in books or on film isn't enough, however. Seeing these masterpieces and experiencing the history and relics of Rome in person would be a dream come true. Although this is one trip that will take a lot more planning and preparation to become possible, my parents know what it means to me and they'll work with me to make it happen.

Chapter 29

My mom has worked tirelessly to make "wish-list" items come true for me. I feel blessed that this loving, kind, and patient person is my mom. Sure, there are days when I think "Really, mom, you want me to do that?" Or I get upset because she will not let me do or watch something I *desperately* want to watch. As a teenager, however, I guess that's the way it's supposed to be and my aggravation never lasts long. These once-in-a-lifetime experiences my mom has helped create for me have been remarkable, but the moments I share with my mom have also greatly impacted my life.

First is our Good Friday sunrise. It's a unique time and my "mom time." For seven years, mom and I get up bright and early each Good Friday to watch the sunrise. No matter the weather we walk to the beach to watch the sun come up over the horizon. I look forward to this day every year. We take a blanket, spread it out on the sand, sit down, and for the first few minutes we sit in total quiet. There are usually only a few people there, with some fishing and some meditating. We never really talk about anything in particular. It's about just spending quality time together. Mom always has the camera ready and takes what seems like about a hundred pictures to capture and remember the day.

Our second tradition started when I was very young. I can't remember exactly when, but I remember that I needed a stool to reach the counter. It's not something that I've told many people about because, being a guy, I thought others might make fun of me. Every Christmas my great-grandma used to make her traditional red velvet cake. Mom calls it Minnie's red velvet cake, as it is naturally named after her grandma. We make the cake each Christmas Eve. Mom explains that Minnie's cake is different from all other red velvet cakes because of her special ingredients, and more importantly, her signature green icing, which accents the red center and the colors of Christmas.

My mom and I have a lot of fun baking the cake. We usually manage to get cake batter all over the kitchen by the time we're done. Each time we make the cake we hold our breath, hoping this time it will turn out perfectly. More often than not it's a little lopsided, but that just makes it more special. It's really about the time we spend together making the cake than about the outcome.

My dad and I share some special traditions too. When I was younger, we would go to a local airport to watch the planes land, ride the lawnmower together, or play golf. He devotes so much of his time to me and making sure that I am healthy. As I have gotten older, we still play golf but now we enjoy going out to lunch together, watching movies, going to the beach, and watching English soccer.

My dad is my stronghold. He is the one who stays on top of new research for my condition, and he never stops making sure that I am as healthy as I can be. My mom has often shared stories with me about being in the hospital and how dad was always at my side. He is the one who I cling to for guidance in everyday life, especially now that I am older. There is not a day that goes by that my dad doesn't tell me that he loves me; sometimes he tells me three to four times a day. He says I'm the love of his life. I know that his words are true, because his actions speak love each day.

My mom has always been there for me as well, even before I was born. I've heard stories about when I was in the hospital and how hard it was for my family. I know it was tough on my dad, but he's strong, iron-willed, and relentless. My mom and I suffered together. I was suffering physically, and she was suffering on the inside. Every day I am grateful that she didn't leave or give up on me, just like Mary stood by her son's side through his suffering. I think Mary must have been there helping me and my mom too.

Chapter 30

John Paul's Journal

March 29, 2010

I had a good dream last night. I dreamed that I saw Our Lady. She was dressed in blue and white. She had a pretty face. When I saw her I said, "Hail Mary full of grace. She came closer. I said, "Hello Mary." She responded, "Hello John Paul." It was a dream but yet so real. I saw her. Wait until dad hears about this. It happened on his birthday. This is the third time! I will never forget this as long as I live. I know Our Lady will always be here to help me.

I have a very special devotion to Mary, especially Our Lady of Fatima. I love the movie, *The Miracle of Our Lady of Fatima*, which tells the story of Mary as she appeared to three children in Fatima in 1917. Mary asked them to return on the thirteenth of each month and offer their sufferings to God for the salvation of sinners, and to pray the Rosary for world peace. The townspeople didn't believe the children. Our Lady, however, promised a sign that made believers out of nonbelievers on October 13. About 40,000 people showed up on the date in the pouring rain. At noon, the clouds parted and the sun shone brightly, and then the sun moved through a rainbow and seemed to fall to the ground, but finally returned back to the sky. This has been called the Miracle of the Sun.

The reason that I feel this special connection to Our Lady of Fatima is because this title of Our Lady portrays Mary exactly as I picture her: loving, kind, serene, and the protector of children.

Chapter 31

John Paul's Journal

June 3, 2013

Tomorrow is my nineteenth birthday. I have and will devote my life to Christ and try to follow St. Padre Pio and the Little Way of St. Thérèse of Lisieux. I'm excited for my mission to begin. My family encourages me. My parents have worked hard all their lives. They have really helped me, and they are the reason I am where I am today. In my daily religious life, it is my parents who have shaped me to be a good person. I love them. God is my eternal Father, and Mary is my eternal mother. I thank them both for my earthly dad and mom.

My ultimate goal is to become a Catholic priest. Since I was very young, I have felt called to become a priest, to be God's servant on earth and serving those in need. I cherish this vocation and yearn to live a simple life, accepting the vows and commitment. Although I haven't entered seminary yet, I know there are realistic concerns for my becoming a priest due to my disability.

Am I too short to be a priest? Will an order be hesitant in accepting me because of my disability? These questions began playing over and over in my mind about four years ago. It's hard to put into words how I feel as I ponder these questions.

My first thought is that we constantly pray in church for vocations, for young men and women to hear and accept their calling. If that's the prayer the congregation is praying to God, is it wrong for me to think that my disability will create a roadblock in God answering their prayers? I know I am being led by God. I must trust that God will also lift me over my obstacles.

John Paul's Journal

April 4, 2011

You know, sixteen years ago I was supposed to die....
God saved me! Why? Well, I have come to figure out why;
he wants me to join the priesthood. A couple of nights
ago I dreamed of the Eucharist. I was holding up his
body, which was small and a brilliant gold color, saying:
"For this is my Body, which will be given up for you."
Could this be a sign? I think so.

Chapter 32

When I think about entering a vocation to the religious life, the advantages outnumber the disadvantages. The more I grow the stronger my desire to know, love, and serve God grows. That is the true advantage of my vocation, and in doing so, I am able to help others in their spiritual journey.

In discerning my vocation to religious life, I didn't need an airplane to write a message in the sky letting me know my vocation. God defined my calling twenty years ago when I was born with half a heart. The doctors said that I would not live, but with God's help, I did. Sure, there have been twists and turns in my life, and I still encounter obstacles each day, but I believe my purpose is to cherish life as a gift by serving God and others.

There was a particular night when I wasn't feeling quite like myself. When I'm not feeling 100 percent, I like having my dad around because he has a calming effect on me. However, Dad wasn't at home but was in Las Vegas at an apparel show. The stomach pain started out as mild cramps, but then it intensified. I didn't want to worry Mom, so I tried to manage through it at first. I realized that the pain wasn't getting any better. Nausea began to settle in, and I became nervous. With my heart condition there is always a possibility that feeling bad is more than just something simple, and all the possibilities cause me to be anxious. Mom immediately noticed the pain I was in and tried to help me settle down, but nothing seemed to help. Suddenly, I started to get physically sick. Once it started, I couldn't stop. I had never felt this way and I was afraid, especially with Dad being away. I listened as Mom phoned Dad and told him what was happening. I knew she was nervous because she usually doesn't want to worry Dad while he's so far away, but she needed the comfort of his voice. She called my grandparents and asked them to come over, and next I heard her speaking to the doctor. After she spoke to the doctor she seemed more relaxed.

The intense pain lasted for what seemed like forever. For some reason, during this time, I couldn't help but think of Jesus and his suffering on the cross. My pain was so minor in comparison to his, but the reflection put my suffering in perspective. I watched as Mom sent out a text to her friends requesting special prayers for me. It is unbelievable, but not long after the request was sent, the pain began to subside. In reality, I guess it isn't that unbelievable, because it's the power of prayer!

I have been so blessed in my life. I can't help but feel that I must pay forward my blessings to others. I do have a desire to become a priest, which will help me bless others through my service to God and the Eucharist. I am well aware that my illness has influenced my desire. First and foremost, God has allowed me to live, defying the astronomical odds stacked against me. Not only has God given me the gift of life but also he has given me the gift of loving, kind, and generous parents. I believe that God gifted me to my parents because they are special people. He knew my parents would not falter in their beliefs or in their love for me. It doesn't stop with my parents, but continues to my family, friends, and all those who surround me with their love, prayers, and compassion.

Chapter 33

I have to admit that I was a little nervous starting my life as a college student. I had never really been in a traditional school environment. I guess I have been somewhat sheltered, but now it's time to begin my adventure into adulthood. I am secure with who I am, but that doesn't mean I'm not concerned about how others will treat me.

I got a preview of what to expect when I went to see one of my advisors with my mom. Mom explained that I would be beginning classes on Monday. I watch the advisor's mouth drop open with confusion. She questions my mom several times to make sure she is serious and to make sure that I was really starting college.

Mom doesn't miss a beat. She's used to all the questions about my age, just like I am. We enter the advisor's office and mom explains that, yes, I am twenty years old and I am starting college. She also kindly explains that those expressions of disbelief and questions are things I live with daily. Then Mom explains my story in full detail.

After the advisor has heard my story her expression changes. She tells me that based on my personality and smile, I will have no trouble fitting in. Her words are comforting, but I know that when I walk into the classroom, I'm going to get looks and I know those looks will continue wherever I go. The reality is that this "stigma" is going to follow me throughout my life.

Chapter 34

The greatest obstacle that I've had to overcome in my life has been my illness and disability, but when I was younger I never thought about having a disability or even realized that I was different. As I got older, the realization that I was different became more apparent and I had to deal with it. To be frank, I was not happy. I didn't want to be different. I wanted to be like everyone else. I recognized that I had to own my disability instead of hiding from it. I had to come to terms with being disabled. At first it was easier because my disability was hidden. The only visible sign was the long scar down the center of my chest, which I could hide under my clothing. As time moved on, though, I kept getting older but wasn't growing.

Coming to terms with my disability has enabled me to help others who, even though they don't have the exact same problem, can relate to certain feelings of helplessness or being different. I have learned to own who I am and how to deal with the struggles and fears of being different. You do not have to have a disability to have these kinds of fears and struggles. I know that if I had attended a traditional school, I would have encountered the same obstacles many teenagers face today. I'm sure my size would have been an issue, and that I would have been considered "not normal" by a lot of my classmates. I can only imagine how those who are singled out as different feel and cope with that anxiety.

Yes, I own my disability. I am different. I am living with half a heart. It's not just that I look short for my age. I look eleven even though I'm twenty. I go into a restaurant and am automatically offered crayons and a kid's menu. Of course I still feel belittled, but I've learned to politely decline instead of trying to explain my condition. I do have days when I feel trapped in this small body, unable to do certain things, but that's OK. I don't blame anyone. That's what makes me special, what makes me John Paul. I am just happy to be alive and doing the will of God. I thank him for allowing me to be in the world and giving me the opportunity to use my experiences to help others.

We are all different and unique. God made us that way so that each of us would be special, an individual. Others may make us feel being "not normal" is a bad thing, but we are all normal and equal in God's eyes. That's the beauty of being ourselves!

I can't change who I am, but I can change the world as I am.

John Paul's Prayer

*Oh sweet Jesus, you are the sun in the morning that rises
and enters me each day through the Holy Eucharist.
I pray that I will fulfill your mission as a priest. You are
all I need, nothing else. I am deeply in love with Christ.
Show me to you, sweet Jesus, and I will deny myself,
take up my cross, and follow you.*

Epilogue

In Gratitude

I am fortunate to have this venue to convey my thanks. I have to admit that I thought this epilogue would be the easiest to write, but for some reason it has been difficult. The title itself, "In Gratitude," is simple. Gratitude is usually expressed with two words, thank you. In reality there is no way that I can express my sincere gratitude to all those who have been involved in John Paul's life for the past twenty years. There have been so many people who have come in and out of our lives during this time. As I have mentioned many times, it is amazing how God places appropriate people in our lives at the appropriate time.

I believe that people are sent into our lives for a purpose. I received an email not long ago that made me think more about this. People come into your life for a reason, for a season, or for a lifetime. When someone enters your life for a reason, it is usually to meet a need. They may come to assist you during a difficult time to provide guidance and support, be it emotionally or spiritually. When our desire is fulfilled, their work done, and the prayer you sent up answered, they move on. Some people come into your life for a season, because your turn has come to share, grow, and learn. They may give you peace, make you laugh, or teach you something. They give you unbelievable joy, but only for a season. Lifetime relationships teach lifetime lessons, that is, things to build on in order to have a solid emotional foundation. Your job is to accept the lesson, love the person, and put the knowledge gained into other relationships and areas of your life. After reading this, I thought about all the people who entered my family's life in the past twenty years. Some have been there for a reason, some for a season, and some for a lifetime. It is because of each individual's unique love, friendship, and prayer that John Paul is with us today. This epilogue is dedicated to all the people who have nourished John Paul through prayer, kindness, love, and dedication.

First and foremost I thank God for giving Annette and me our most precious gift, John Paul. If I were to say thank you every second of every day it would not be enough. It is only by the grace of God that John Paul lives. It is not only during the trying times that God's presence is felt but also on a daily basis. Annette feels that same presence. Our faith is strengthened with every passing day. Sure there are valleys, but the valleys must be traveled in order to make it to the mountaintops.

I say thank you to the Blessed Mother for her intercession. Thank you to all the guardian angels and saints, especially St. Padre Pio, whose presence we experienced on numerous occasions in some of our darkest hours by that sweet scent of a rose.

Writing this book I have relived events that have been secluded in the recesses of my mind for many years. Dredging through these memories has been difficult. Maybe that is why I waited so long. I did not impulsively decide I was going to write a book about John Paul. It is much deeper than that. The memory is still vivid. During John Paul's hospital stay for the third stage, Annette and I were sitting on a cushioned bench in the breezeway of the floor of the PICU. I began to think about John Paul and all the miracles that had taken place in his short life. I prayed for another miracle, and in that prayer I made a vow. The vow was to write a memoir of John Paul's life and share the many miracles God bestowed on him and my family.

During this journey I have come into contact with many families who are enduring their own nightmare of having a sick child. I dedicate this book to each of them. Most not only have to deal with this dreadful nightmare but also the day-to-day struggles of maintaining the family. I encourage anyone who is having a rough day, feeling desolate, or down on their luck to visit the hospital. Take a walk down the corridors of the pediatric unit. See the children suffering from cancer, heart problems, or any illness. I guarantee after passing a few doors that your attitude will change.

In life there are interruptions. I have survived and am still surviving a serious interruption. Through this book I hope you have gained a positive perspective to always believe in hope even when you are told there is no hope, to never give up, to hold steadfast to faith, fortitude, and perseverance, and to remember the importance of being an advocate for those you love. Last but not least, embrace the precious and greatest gift of all, the gift of life. For life is a gift, one to be cherished and preserved.

There are many people to thank when it comes to writing this book. I begin with my son, John Paul, the love of my life. Thank you for blessing my life each day.

And to my wife, Annette, for your dedication and unending assistance, without whom this book would never have been possible.

To our parents, Tommy and Robena, and Dolour and Lette, thanks for being our solid ground during the many mountains and valleys that have marked our journey.

To Cecilia, Fr. Gary, and Gerard, my siblings, thanks for your constant faith, reassurance, and always being there.

And in memory of Annette's sister and brother, Debbie and Barry, who through their actions taught me the attribute of fortitude and the magnitude of a smile.

Thanks to all the people who have touched John Paul's life in their own special way, including the Kirsch, McKinney, Summers, Mundie, Pierce, and Schindler families; Tyler Perry; Carole Wurst; Eirk Compton; Coach Ream; Don Smith; Jack Nicklaus; Jane Seymour; Michael Clayton; Tiffany Beasley; Kathy Brown; Dr. Bayron; Father O'Shea; Chrissi Deutsch; Debbie Guinn; the Friday morning breakfast group; our Passionist priests; Rachel Boland of Moments and Milestones Photography for the amazing cover photo; all of our families and friends; and the many people who prayed and continue to pray for John Paul around the world.

Thanks to our parish priests, our daily Mass friends, our agent Doug Corcoran, our editor Theresa Nienaber, and the wonderful people at Liguori Publications. Thanks also to Don Imus and the *Imus in the Morning* radio crew, EWTN's Doug Keck, Jim and Joy, Ken Langone, Cindy Rosa, Kathy Jorden, Kitty Honeycutt, Rosaline Klaben, Joyce O'Neill, and Robin Huggett, and News Corporation's Bobby Butler.

And finally, thanks to everyone else who is a part of John Paul's life. Each of you has made such a positive impact.

Derek George

SNAPSHOTS OF JOHN PAUL, FAMILY, AND FRIENDS

President Barack Obama
with Derek, Annette, and John Paul George

Best-selling author James Patterson stops by the
book-signing table after the original edition of
Heart of a Lion is published.

Actress Jane Seymour

Bobby Butler
of News Corporation

Television's
Natalie Morales

Radio's Don Imus

Golfer Tiger Woods

Entertainer Tyler Perry